Writing an Applied I
Thesis or Disser

Writing an Applied Linguistics Thesis or Dissertation

A Guide to Presenting Empirical Research

JOHN BITCHENER

First published 2010 by
RED GLOBE PRESS

Red Globe Press in the UK is an imprint of Springer Nature Limited,
registered in England, company number 785998, of 4 Crinan Street,
London, N1 9XW.

Red Globe Press® is a registered trademark in the United States,
the United Kingdom, Europe and other countries.

ISBN 978–0–230–22454–4   ISBN 978–1–137–04337–5 (eBook)

This book is printed on paper suitable for recycling and made from fully
managed and sustained forest sources. Logging, pulping and manufacturing
processes are expected to conform to the environmental regulations
of the country of origin.

A catalogue record for this book is available from the British Library.

A catalog record for this book is available from the Library of Congress.

Contents

Preface

This book has been written in response to frequently asked questions by first time thesis writers about (1) the content that is relevant to different parts of a thesis, (2) how the content can be most effectively organized and (3) the extent to which the various sections of a thesis have particular language and presentational characteristics. Each of these issues is discussed in relation to the typical part-genres of an empirically based thesis: the abstract, the introduction, the literature review, the methodology, the results, the discussion of results and the conclusion. The focus of the book is therefore on the writing up of the thesis rather than on the research process.

The book will be of interest to a wide audience. The main target group is first-time writers of an empirically based thesis. To varying extents, it will also have relevance to writers of other thesis types. Secondly, although the illustrative material presented in the book has been drawn from theses in Applied Linguistics, this does not mean that it is only relevant for those working within this discipline. Any student writing up a piece of empirical research, particularly but not exclusively with a social science orientation, will find the book instructive. Thirdly, the book has been written for both native and second language speakers of English. Finally, it is anticipated that the book will also be useful for thesis supervisors and for training units within tertiary institutions preparing supervisors and others for the task ahead.

The book comprises eight chapters: the background to the book, the abstract, the introduction, the literature review, the methodology, the results, the discussion of results and the conclusion. After the background chapter, each of the following chapters covers the same areas of content and presents it in the same way across chapters:

- Introduction to the chapter
- Purpose/functions of the part-genre (chapter)

- Content and structure options for the part-genre (chapter)
- Linguistic and presentational characteristics of the part-genre (chapter)
- Frequently asked questions and answers
- Further activities
- Further reading

The content and structure section of each chapter considers a number of options for deciding upon the units of content that could be included and for deciding how these can be most effectively organized. Throughout, excerpts from a sample thesis are presented to illustrate the options presented. This is then followed up with a detailed commentary on what has been included by the author and on the extent to which the various options have been incorporated into her thesis.

The material in this book can be used a variety of ways. At an individual level, students can either read the whole through from cover to cover or dip into various chapters depending on where they are at in the writing process. Thus, it can be used as a reference guide. Supervisors might find this option particularly useful. The book can also be used in classes, seminars and workshops as a core text or as a resource tool to accompany other materials. Used in these ways, the further activities sections will provide teachers and presenters with ready-made tasks for student/trainee use. Those interested in the research that underpins the content will find plenty of suggestions at the end of each chapter for further reading. Other uses of the book will no doubt be identified by its users over time.

In no way is the material presented in the book intended to be prescriptive. The approach that has been taken is one that presents options that might be considered by individual thesis writers. The options included in the book are based on discourse analysis research of typical approaches that have been taken in the writing of the various part-genres and on feedback from supervisors and students about what they have found to be helpful advice. It is hoped that you, as readers of this book, will find the material equally helpful.

Acknowledgements

This book would not have been possible without the permission of Katherine Cao whose first class Master's thesis has been used to illustrate most of the material presented in this book. Katherine's thesis won the Applied Linguistics Association of New Zealand Best Master's thesis competition two years ago not only for the quality of the content of the thesis but also for the way in which it had been so clearly and effectively written. I am also grateful to Shawn Loewen for allowing me to refer to his Doctoral abstract so that points of comparison could be made between his and Katherine's approach to this part-genre. Much of the inspiration for writing the book came from staff and students at both my own university and other universities in New Zealand, Australia, the United States and Asia. Without the insight of Madeline Banda, Director of Postgraduate Studies at AUT University and key members of her team like Annette Tiaiti, the seminar and workshop series on thesis writing that informed the focus of the book would not have been offered and the book's content may have not been field-tested. Student feedback on these seminars and workshops identified where their needs lay and so played a major role in determining the content of the book. I am grateful to all the students I have supervised over the last decade for the way in which they challenged me to articulate precisely what was required when writing the different parts of their thesis. Meeting these demands forced me to reflect upon the recurrent issues facing first time thesis writers and upon how they might be most effectively addressed. Over the years, many of my New Zealand and international colleagues had suggested that I put into print what they had heard me say at conferences and during informal conversations about effective thesis writing. In this regard, I am especially grateful to Professor Dana Ferris (University of California, Davis) and Professor Margie Berns (Purdue University) for their inspiration and insightful comments on an early draft of the book. Without the additional comments and suggestions of the anonymous reviewers of the book, a number of the refinements that appear in the book would not have been included. Last, but not least, I wish to acknowledge the support and clear guidance given by Kitty van Boxel and the team at Palgrave Macmillan. They have been so pleasant and easy to work with over the past year.

1 Background

WHAT IS THE BOOK ABOUT?

This book has been written to introduce first-time thesis and dissertation (hereafter, 'thesis' rather than 'dissertation' will be used) writers to the process of writing up an empirically based piece of research. It has three key aims. The first is to introduce you to the type of content that is typically presented in each of the part-genres (chapters or sections) of a thesis: the abstract, the introduction, the literature review, the methodology, the results, the discussion and the conclusion. The second aim is to introduce a range of options for presenting or structuring your content so that it is rhetorically and persuasively effective. The third aim is to acquaint you with some of the key linguistic and presentation features of each part-genre so that your content is presented with clarity, coherence and cohesion. Thus, the book has been written to help you with the writing-up process rather than the research process.

WHO IS THE BOOK FOR?

The book has been written to address the three key areas identified above for students writing their first thesis, usually at Masters or Honours level, but it may also be of value to Doctoral students who have not previously completed a thesis. It may also be of value to supervisors and those offering thesis-writing course-work papers/courses, seminars, workshops or other forms of preparatory training because it provides content and worked analyses of sections of each of the chapters written by a first-time thesis writer. Unlike some thesis-writing texts, this book has been written to cater to the needs of both native speakers of English as well as to those who have an ESL (English as a Second Language) or

EFL (English as a Foreign Language) background. Although the book focuses on approaches that are characteristic of theses in Applied Linguistics, students, in other disciplines, who are writing up a piece of empirically based research (irrespective of whether it is quantitative or qualitative in focus) will also find the book helpful because the book adopts an approach that trains you as reader to analyze other theses within or outside the field of Applied Linguistics.

WHY HAS THE BOOK BEEN WRITTEN?

The book has been written to meet the needs of students who say they are unsure or unaware of the specific part-genre content and organizational expectations and requirements of supervisors, institutions and examiners. Sometimes, students also mention that they want to know more about how the content should be formatted and expressed. These issues, from both supervisor and student perspectives, have been reported in a range of published articles and texts. In first presenting seminars and workshops to first-time thesis writers in the UK, USA, Australia and New Zealand, I was surprised to find so many students attending these non-credit-bearing sessions. However, it soon became clear that some of the sources from which supervisors and others expected their students to have gained an understanding of these requirements and expectations were not actually focusing their attention on the content and organizational detail that students were wanting. For example, as a student preparing to do a major piece of research, you are likely to have completed a research methods course but it may not have been one that focused on the specific content and organizational characteristics of different parts of the thesis. As a student, you may also have consulted some of the available guidebooks and handbooks on how to write a thesis and not found them particularly informative about the type of content that is relevant to the part-genres or about ways of effectively structuring the content. This is not so much a criticism of the available practitioner advice as a reflection of their different aims and purpose. Many are focused on aspects of the research process and on an overview of the macro-structure of a thesis rather than on the micro-elements of the part-genres.

Another reason for reading this book may be that you have not yet had any discussion with your supervisor about the various part-genres. Sometimes, students have also said that their supervisor's tacit understanding of what is required is not articulated explicitly enough with examples for their full understanding. If you are reading this book for any of these reasons, you should feel that your specific needs have been met by the time you have read the material in this book and sought to apply what has been presented. The material has been field-tested over a number of years and has been positively received internationally by students from different ethnic, language and educational backgrounds.

HOW DOES THE BOOK MEET THE CONTENT, STRUCTURE, LINGUISTIC AND PRESENTATIONAL NEEDS OF STUDENTS?

To help you understand what content and structure are appropriate for the different parts of your thesis, the book presents a range of options, illustrating them with analyses of and commentary on a range of sections from the part-genres of a well-written Masters thesis in Applied Linguistics. The approach taken in the book is drawn from genre analytic research and best practice supervisor advice. Because the content is research informed, we need to consider why the genre approach is relevant to the needs of students writing their first thesis.

Examining the discourse of a genre, like the thesis and its part-genres, enables us to understand the type of content that is typically presented and how it is presented so that the narrative or argument or case that is being presented is accomplished with rhetorical effectiveness. The starting point of this justification is an understanding of what a genre is. The term 'genre' has been defined in a variety of ways but, in each full definition, several key characteristics tend to be present. The first characteristic is that a genre is a type of discourse that occurs in a particular setting. In this case, the particular setting is an academic setting where the expectations and requirements of what constitutes a thesis are defined by the academic community of researchers, teachers, examiners, supervisors and institutions. The second characteristic is that a genre has distinctive and recognizable patterns and norms with respect to content and structure. In other words, the type of content and structure that you observe in one thesis will be sufficiently similar to that observed in other theses. The third characteristic is that it has particular and distinctive communicative functions and these determine the nature of the content and how it is organized. Consequently, each of the chapters of your thesis will meet different requirements and expectations. So, having defined the key elements of a genre and indicated the relevance of the genre analytic approach taken in this book, we can now consider the relationship between these characteristics and how analytic research has informed our understanding of what constitutes a part-genre.

Genre theory has proposed and genre research has revealed (1) how the purpose or functions of a genre or part-genre inform the choice of content and its rhetorical staging or organization and (2) how this staging can be identified in terms of the discourse moves (separate units/sections of content) and sub-moves (also referred to in the literature as steps or strategies) that are employed. (If you are interested in reading some of the literature on this topic, a list of further reading suggestions is provided at the end of this chapter.) Because of these relationships, it is important that you understand first the various functions of each part-genre as these will determine what content and structure is relevant. Therefore, each of the chapters in this book will focus on a different part-genre and each will begin with an outline of its purpose and functions. This will be followed up with a consideration of the type of content that might be presented and, in doing so, focus on how it can be effectively presented. First, you will be introduced to a range of optional moves and sub-moves. Each move and sub-move will then be illustrated with extracts from our sample Masters thesis. Key features about the way in which the author has made use of the various options will be discussed. It will be emphasized throughout the book that the moves and sub-moves presented in each chapter are options; they are not a prescriptive list that you must use. Although you may choose to use all of the options, you do not need to feel constrained by the range presented. Depending on the topic and focus of your thesis, you may be able to add other moves or sub-moves.

HOW IS THE BOOK ORGANIZED?

The book comprises eight chapters with the following seven chapters being devoted to a separate part-genre of the thesis. Although each of these chapters considers a different part-genre, authors sometimes include more than one part-genre in a single chapter. For instance, the discussion of results is sometimes combined with a presentation of the results and sometimes the discussion of results is combined with the conclusion. In contrast, the literature review part-genre is sometimes spread across more than one chapter. If you are presenting more than one part-genre in a single chapter or spreading a part-genre across more than one chapter, the approach taken in this book can easily be adapted.

Within each chapter of this book, the areas of focus are the same. After an introduction, we will consider the purpose and functions of the part-genre. This is followed by an outline of the moves and sub-moves that can be employed in the presentation of content. The extent to which these moves and sub-moves are employed and the way in which they are organized is then illustrated from our sample Masters thesis. The decisions that have been made about the content and the organizational patterns of this material are then discussed. You will note that the analyses are presented in two columns: the first presents the text and the second the move analysis. Where a move has not been presented alongside a sentence, it means that the same move employed in the previous sentence has again been used. Having read the material, there will be opportunities for you to apply it in move and sub-move analyses as you proceed through the chapter and in the further activities section presented towards the end of the chapter. Some of the linguistic features that often characterize the part-genre under consideration are then presented and illustrated. On a few occasions, presentational features are also discussed. Following this material, answers to frequently asked questions are provided. These are not intended to be necessarily definitive or exhaustive but intended rather as guidelines that you can discuss with your supervisor. A further activities section provides you with additional opportunities to apply what you have been reading. You may find it helpful to work on these activities with a fellow student or with your supervisor.

Each chapter ends with a list of references for further reading. You will find these worthwhile if you are interested in what others have said about thesis-writing and in what the published research informing this book has discovered. Finally, all the moves presented in the various chapters are given in an appendix at the end of the book.

WHAT IS THE SAMPLE MASTERS THESIS ABOUT AND WHY HAS IT BEEN SELECTED?

Throughout the book, illustrations will be drawn from one Masters thesis. For the sake of clarity, the decision was made to focus on one area of content rather than on a range of areas and to select one that was well written and that illustrated many of the features typically found in empirically based theses. Because you will be learning how to analyze extracts of discourse, you will be able to apply what you have learned to other texts and theses. Therefore, if your literature search has led you to theses in your area of investigation, you will be able to analyze what they have presented and how the content has been organized. These observations may then guide the decisions that you make about what to include in your thesis and about how to present your material in an effective manner.

The sample thesis that we will be referring to in this book was written by a very able Masters student who has since gone on to complete a Doctoral thesis in the same field of enquiry. The Masters thesis is entitled 'Willingness to communicate in a second language classroom'. The thesis investigates the willingness of second language learners of English to communicate in a second language learning classroom. It examines whether their willingness to take part in interactive activities is determined by innate trait-like factors and/or situation-specific factors, including participation in pair work, small group interactions and plenary discussions. The subject matter of the thesis is reasonably accessible for those not familiar with the area. Inevitably, a certain amount of jargon specific to the field is presented so in Chapter 2 on the thesis abstract, key terms and construct are glossed. If you are not reading the book in chapter sequence, you may need to refer to the abstract chapter in case some of the material requires clarification. Having said this, however, the content that is presented should be easily understood even if some of the terminology in the illustrative examples is not familiar to you.

HOW CAN THIS BOOK BE USED?

The book can be used in a variety of ways. First and foremost, it was written as a reference guide for students who are about to start writing various parts of their thesis. As such, you could skim read it to get an idea of what is presented or to find out about a particular aspect of the writing process. For example, you may want to see what information has been provided on the functions of a literature review in order to check whether or not you have a clear enough understanding of its purpose and functions. Once you are about to start writing a particular chapter, you may want to read that particular part of the book more closely.

Supervisors may also find the book useful if they want to access some already prepared material about any of the part-genres of a thesis. Rather than having to reinvent the wheel, supervisors may find it a ready tool to use with their students. The further activities section may provide a good basis for dialogue between supervisors and their students.

The material in the book can also be used by seminar and work-shop presenters. Already this has been the case in institutions that offer introductory, common-core programmes for their students, where generic content, that can be applied to any discipline, is presented. The material in the book could also be adapted for discipline-specific courses.

Undergraduate teachers (for example, those offering academic writing courses and research methods and presentation courses) may also find parts of the book helpful. Both the instructional and analytical material can be presented in a classroom environment and students can be given opportunities to use the further activities section of each chapter to further apply what they have learned.

Thus, there is a multiplicity of ways in which the book can be used in any discipline. The material has been field-tested in seminars and workshops with thesis/dissertation students in a wide range of disciplines across universities in Canada, USA, Australia and New Zealand.

FURTHER READING

Belcher, D. (1994). The apprenticeship approach to advanced academic literacy: Graduate students and their mentors. *English for Specific Purposes, 13*, 23–34.

Bitchener, J., & Basturkmen, H. (2006). Perceptions of the difficulties of postgraduate L2 thesis students writing the discussion section. *Journal of English for Academic Purposes, 5*, 4–18.

Casanave, C., & Hubbard, P. (1992). The writing assignments and writing problems of doctoral students: Faculty perceptions, pedagogical issues, and needed research. *English for Specific Purposes, 11*, 33–49.

Cheng, A. (2007). Transferring generic features and recontextualizing genre awareness: Understanding writing performance in the ESP genre-based literacy framework. *English for Specific Purposes, 26*, 287–307.

Cooley, L., & Lewkowicz, J. (1997). Developing awareness of the rhetorical and linguistic conventions of writing a thesis in English: Addressing the needs of ESL/EFL postgraduate students. In A. Duszak (Ed.) *Culture and Styles of Academic Discourse* (pp. 113–140). Berlin: Mouton de Gruyter.

Devitt, A. (2004). *Writing Genres (Rhetorical Philosophy and Theory)*. Carbondale: Southern Illinois University Press.

Devitt, A., Reiff, M., & Bawarshi, A. (2004). *Scenes of Writing: Strategies for Composing with Genres*. New York: Pearson/Longman.

Dong, Y. (1998). Non-native graduate students' thesis/dissertation writing in science: Self-reports by students and their advisors from two US institutions. *English for Specific Purposes, 17*, 369–390.

Dudley-Evans, T. (1993). Variation in communication patterns between discourse communities: The case of Highway Engineering and Plant Biology. In G. Blue (Ed.), *Language, Learning and Success Studying Through English* (pp. 141–147). London: Macmillan Publishers.

Hopkins, A., & Dudley-Evans, T. (1988). A genre-based investigation of the discussion section in articles and dissertations. *English for Specific Purposes, 7*, 113–121.

Hyland, K. (2000). *Disciplinary Discourses: Social Interactions in Academic Writing*. London: Pearson Education.

Jenkins, S., Jordan, M., & Weiland, P. (1993). The role of writing in graduate engineering education: A survey of faculty beliefs and practices. *English for Specific Purposes, 12,* 51–67.

Paltridge, B. (2002). Thesis and dissertation writing: An examination of published advice and actual practice. *English for Specific Purposes, 21,* 125–143.

Paltridge, B., & Starfield, S. (2007). *Thesis and Dissertation Writing in a Second Language: A Handbook for Supervisors.* New York: Routledge.

Samraj, B. (2008). A discourse analysis of master's theses across disciplines with a focus on introductions. *Journal of English for Academic Purposes, 7,* 55–67.

Swales, J. (2004). *Research Genres: Exploration and Applications.* Cambridge: Cambridge University Press.

2 Abstract

INTRODUCTION

In this chapter, we are going to look at the type of content that may be included in a thesis abstract and at how it can be organized. But first, we need to consider the purpose or function of an abstract. Having done that, we will focus on the content areas typically included in a thesis abstract and on the ways in which this material may be presented effectively. We will then analyze an abstract written by a Masters student and compare it with another by a Doctoral student. The analyses provided in the chapter of this book will be a little more extensive than those in other chapters so that, if you are reading this chapter before others, you will have a clear and detailed understanding of the analytical approach that informs the book. This will be followed up with a discussion of one of the key linguistic features of thesis abstracts. The chapter will close with answers to some frequently asked questions, with some further activities and a list of readings that will introduce you to some of the literature informing the material presented in this chapter.

THE FUNCTIONS OF A THESIS ABSTRACT

The key aim of a thesis abstract is to introduce the reader to the main considerations of the thesis so most often include the functions presented below in Box 2a.

Box 2a   Functions of a thesis abstract

1. The aims of the study
2. The background and context of the study

---

3. The methodology and methods used in the study
4. The key findings of the study
5. The contribution of the study to the field of knowledge

To some extent, it also has a persuasive function, namely, to convince readers that the main text has something new and important to offer. In the next section, we will look at the type of content that may be presented in an abstract and of ways of effectively structuring it. In doing so, you will see how both the content and its organization are determined by the functions of an abstract.

THE CONTENT AND STRUCTURE OF A THESIS ABSTRACT

You will recall, in Chapter 1, that we discussed the role that genre analysis has played in helping writers understand (1) the type and structure of content that typically characterize the different part-genres of a thesis and (2) how this may be achieved through the use of various moves (units of content) and sub-moves (steps or strategies that are used in the presentation of the units of content). In this section, we are going to consider the range of move and sub-move options that you can choose from when writing a thesis abstract.

Box 2b   Abstract move and sub-move options

Moves	Sub-moves
1. Introduction	a. Provide context, background of the research
	b. Identify the motivation for the research
	c. Explain the significance/centrality of the research focus
	d. Identify a research gap or continuation of research tradition
2. Purpose	a. Identify aims or intentions, questions or hypotheses
	b. Develop aims or intentions, questions or hypotheses

Box 2b   (Continued)

Moves	Sub-moves
3. Method	a. Identify/justify overall approach and methods b. Identify key design aspects c. Identify data source(s) and parameters d. Identify data analysis processes
4. Product	a. Present main findings/results of key aims, questions b. Present main findings/results of subsidiary/ additional aims, questions
5. Conclusion	a. Suggest significance/importance of findings beyond the research, considering contributions to theory, research and practice b. Suggest applications (for practice) and implications (for further research)

As you can see from Box 2b above, there are five moves and a range of sub-moves that can be included. The extent to which all of them are included may vary from topic to topic as well as within and across disciplines. When we analyze the abstract from our sample theses in the next two sections, you will see that the author included all five moves and most of the sub-moves. When deciding which moves and sub-moves to include in your thesis, you may wish to discuss the options with your supervisor.

ANALYSIS OF A MASTERS THESIS ABSTRACT

In this section, we will be analyzing the abstract moves and sub-moves employed by the author of our sample Masters thesis (see Chapter 1 for background details on this thesis). Before reading the analysis, I would suggest that you try to identify the moves and sub-moves included in the abstract, using the options given in Box 2b. If you decide to do this, you will be in a better position to understand and respond to the analysis that follows. You can write your moves and sub-moves in the space provided in column two of Box 2c below. Having done this, you can compare your answers with those provided in Box 2d below.

Box 2c   Abstract text and move structure

1. Willingness to communicate, an individual difference variable, is currently receiving an increasing amount of attention in the literature on second language learning. 2. The present study has continued that focus by investigating whether WTC should be considered a trait-like variable, or whether it is more properly regarded as a situational variable. 3. This distinction was drawn by MacIntyre et al. (1998), who posited that WTC in L2 possesses these dual characteristics, different from the trait-like WTC in L1. 4. In essence, the consistency between learners' self-report WTC and their actual WTC behavior in an L2 classroom setting was examined. 5. The study also aimed to look at how WTC varied according to changes in the size of three classroom contexts which entailed both a spatial and temporal dimension – whole class, small groups and dyads – over a one-month period of a language course. 6. A multi-method approach underpinned the study by enabling the construct to be looked at from different perspectives. 7. This approach, involving the adoption of structured classroom observation, participant interviews and questionnaires, overcame the weakness of using self-report survey as a single instrument to examine the multidimensional willingness to communicate construct. 8. Ten students, enrolled in a general English program at an Auckland language school, completed WTC questionnaires. 9. Classroom observation of eight classes (sixteen hours) served as the primary tool to collect data. 10. Follow-up interviews were then conducted with the participants. 11. Findings from the study revealed

---

Box 2c   (Continued)

that WTC in L2 was both a trait-like and a situational-based variable. 12. The trait-level WTC could determine an individual's general tendency in communication whereas state-level WTC predicted the decision to initiate communication within a particular context. 13. As a situational variable, WTC was found to be open to change over time. 14. A number of factors that appeared to influence learners' willingness to communicate behavior in three classroom contexts were identified as: the number of interlocutor(s) in a particular context, familiarity with interlocutor(s), interlocutor(s)' task performance, interest in topics under discussion in tasks, task types for pair/group work, whether L1 or L2 was used as medium of communication and participants' cultural backgrounds. 15. The results of the study contribute to an understanding of the dynamic nature of willingness to communicate in a second language. 16. Practical suggestions for pedagogy and future research were also identified.

Box 2d   Abstract text and move structure analysis

1. Willingness to communicate, an individual difference variable, is currently receiving an increasing amount of attention in the literature on second language learning. 2. The present study has continued that focus by investigating whether WTC should be considered a trait-like variable, or whether it is more properly regarded as a situational variable. 3. This distinction was drawn by MacIntyre et al. (1998), who posited that WTC in L2 possesses these dual

Moves 1a, b
(Introduction – context, motivation)
Moves 1d, 2a
(Introduction – continue tradition; purpose identified)

Move 2b (purpose developed)

characteristics, different from the trait-like WTC in LI. 4. In essence, the consistency between learners' self-report WTC and their actual WTC behavior in an L2 classroom setting was examined. 5. The study also aimed to look at how WTC varied according to changes in the size of three classroom contexts which entailed both a spatial and temporal dimension – whole class, small groups and dyads – over a one-month period of a language course. 6. A multi-method approach underpinned the study by enabling the construct to be looked at from different perspectives. 7. This approach, involving the adoption of structured classroom observation, participant interviews and questionnaires, overcame the weakness of using self-report survey as a single instrument to examine the multidimensional willingness to communicate construct. 8. Ten students, enrolled in a general English program at an Auckland language school, completed WTC questionnaires. 9. Classroom observation of eight classes (sixteen hours) served as the primary tool to collect data. 10. Follow-up interviews were then conducted with the participants. 11. Findings from the study revealed that WTC in L2 was both a trait-like and a situational-based variable. 12. The trait-level WTC could determine an individual's general tendency in communication whereas state-level WTC predicted the decision to initiate communication within a particular context. 13. As a situational variable, WTC was found to be open to change over time. 14. A number of factors that appeared to influence learners' willingness to communicate behavior in three classroom contexts were identified as: the number of interlocutor(s) in a particular context, familiarity with interlocutor(s), interlocutor(s)' task performance, interest in topics under discussion

Moves 2b, 3b (purpose developed; method – design)
Moves 2b, 3b (purpose developed; method – design)

Move 3a (method – approach)

Moves 3a, c (method – justification & data sources)

Move 3c (data source 1 & parameters)

Move 3c (data source 2 & parameters)
Move 3c (method – data source 3)
Move 4a (product – key finding)
Move 4b (product – subsidiary finding)

Move 4b (product – subsidiary finding)
Move 4b (product – subsidiary finding)

> **Box 2d   (Continued)**
>
> in tasks, task types for pair/group work, whether LI or L2 was used as medium of communication and participants' cultural backgrounds. 15. The results of the study contribute to an understanding of the dynamic nature of willingness to communicate in a second language. 16. Practical suggestions for pedagogy and future research were also identified.
>
> Move 5a (conclusion – significance, novelty)
>
> Move 5b (conclusion – application & further research)

Glossary of terms used in the abstract

1. **willingness to communicate**: the extent to which a second language learner is willing to communicate in the classroom
2. **individual difference variable**: willingness to communicate in the classroom is something that varies from one individual to another
3. **trait-like variable**: a learner's general motivational orientation
4. **situational variable**: a learner's situation-specific motives and setting characteristics

Overall patterns

There are three noteworthy features about the way in which the moves and sub-moves have been presented in the abstract:

1. All five moves have been included in the abstract.
2. Some sentences include two moves. This is particularly the case with the first three moves (Introduction, Purpose and Method). When two moves are presented in one sentence, one of the two moves often provides a reason or justification for the other move.
3. The Method move is given more coverage than other moves (sentences 4–10).

The patterns that you choose will reflect the focus that you wish to give in your abstract. For example, you may want to focus on your research method (particularly if it is novel and comprises a variety of approaches) or you may choose to focus on your product (particularly if there was a range of research questions).

Now that we have considered some of the overall patterns, we will focus our attention on the way in which various moves and sub-moves have been presented.

Introduction and Purpose

Sentence 1

This sentence introduces the wider context of the study (the willingness of second language learners to communicate in the language classroom) and points to its importance as a central area of current research interest. Although it is a very general, introductory statement, you can see that it draws our attention to the fact that the willingness to communicate (hereafter referred to as WTC) construct is an area of immediate relevance and interest to researchers and practitioners.

Sentence 2

The author then develops the introductory claim made in sentence 1. The sentence explains the central purpose of this ongoing investigation into WTC: to investigate whether it should be considered a trait-like or situational variable. By explaining that the study has continued the focus referred to in sentence 1, the author is claiming (although somewhat indirectly) that the focus of this study is a new area of investigation. Notice how this opening statement on purpose follows logically from the opening introductory move and provides a clear example of the juxtaposition of two related moves within a single sentence.

Sentence 3

This sentence develops the statement of purpose presented in sentence 2. Although the author does not define either the term 'trait-like variable' or 'situational variable', she does state that the difference between the two terms was distinguished by MacIntyre et al. in earlier work. She then explains their belief that both variables occur in the WTC of second language learners in a way that is different to the WTC of first language learners. By implication, the motivation for examining the two variables in the study is revealed: to investigate the extent to which each is evident in the behaviour of second language learners in a language learning classroom. So, you can see that this sentence has revealed more about the purpose and motivation of the study.

Method

Sentence 4

With the general purpose of the study having been introduced, sentence 4 focuses more closely on its specific aim or purpose. Having implied that there may be a difference in the extent to which the two variables occur in such classroom environments, the author explains that it was therefore important to examine their actual behaviour. The first detail concerning the method that was employed to observe this behaviour is then presented – an observation of classroom behaviour. Without being specific at this point about which method was used, this sentence states that some form of self-report data was a part of the study's wider methodology. You will also see how the author is implying that there may be a difference between what second language learners think they are doing or not doing when it comes to taking an active part in classroom communication and what the observations of their behaviour actually reveal. So, in summary, the sentence has introduced us to both the specific purpose of the study and two aspects of the method that were employed to achieve the purpose.

Sentence 5

Here, the author also begins with a statement of purpose. She clarifies the fact that the purpose of the study was not just to investigate any inconsistency between what students think they are doing and what their observed behaviour reveals but also to examine whether different classroom contexts are likely to play a role in any difference. Thus, she specifically mentions two further aspects of the study's methodology. First, its investigation into whether a difference in WTC might occur as a result of student communication within a whole class setting, within small groups or within dyadic (paired) groupings. Second, she explains that the study was conducted over a 1-month period. So, again, we can see that this sentence links two moves (purpose and method) in order to explain how the particular purpose was investigated.

Sentence 6

Having already presented specific aspects of the methodology that relate to the key purposes of the study and to the context in which it occurred, sentence 6 refers to the wider approach that was taken to investigate the various purposes. This is an introductory statement about the specific methods that are presented in the sentences that follow. You might ask why this broader statement has been given here after earlier specifics on the methods employed in the study and why it is then followed up with further specifics. This is a good question to ask. It is one that might receive different but equally valid and plausible responses from different readers. On the one hand, it might be argued that, in earlier sentences, the author was seeking to link only contextual aspects of the methodology to the statements of purpose so that the reader can immediately understand the contextual parameters of the investigation. On the other hand, it might be argued that a separation of contextual detail from data source detail was desirable in light of the amount of methodology detail being presented in the abstract. Either argument would seem to be reasonable. Thus, it is really a matter of individual preference. But, having said this, the most common practice is one that describes the overall methodological approach before presenting the specific methods that were chosen.

Sentence 7

This sentence introduces us to the types of data that were collected in the study and explains why a multi-method approach was chosen for the study. Following on from sentence 6, we are first told that three types of data were used in the investigation: structured class-room observation, participant interviews and questionnaires. The author then explains that limitations with using a single data source for exploring a multidimensional construct like WTC meant that more than one type of data were used. In particular, she explains that the use of self-report data alone would have been a limitation given the caution mentioned earlier in sentence 4. It is interesting and I believe important to note that the author is juxtaposing a justification for methodological decision that she made. You will see that this occurs elsewhere in the abstract and so enables us to understand why particular decisions were made with all aspects of the study.

Sentence 8

Next, the methodological statement of sentence 7 is introduced. Reference is made to the first of the three data sources (the use of self-report questionnaires) and its parameters: the number (ten) and type of learners (language school) who participated in the study and the specific contextual setting (an Auckland language school). Note again the relevance of the link between both aspects of the methodology (participants and setting) as these are likely to be details of key interest to any reader who, before reading a whole thesis, would want to know whether or not the findings and con-clusions are based on research that is robust and whether or not it is perhaps typical of other, similar research.

Sentence 9

The second data source (classroom observation) and its parameters (observation in 8 classes, totaling 16 hours) are then introduced in sentence 9. The particular importance of this data source is stated and so draws the reader's attention back to earlier sentences about the need for an examination of potentially more reliable data (e.g. classroom observations) than that afforded by self-report questionnaire answers. The limitations of questionnaire findings alone are several but the abstract is not the place to justify decisions that require more lengthy consideration. The methodology chapter of the thesis is the appropriate place for this type of discussion.

Sentence 10

In this sentence, the author concludes the detail on the study's methodology with its brief reference to the third data source: follow-up interviews with participants. This extremely concise statement does not reveal anything else about the interviews so question concerning how many of the observed participants and questionnaire participants were interviewed is not known at this stage. Compared with other statements in the abstract have been presented in more detail, this might be considered a weakness. In many abstracts, overall participant numbers are reported and sometimes this may even include the number who completed questionnaires, who were interviewed and who were observed.

Product

Sentence 11

We are then introduced to the first of four product statements. In keeping with the key aim of the study – to investigate the occurrence of trait-like and situation-based variables in the willingness of second language learners to communicate in their language classrooms – this sentence presents the first key finding of the study (the existence of both variables in their communication behaviour). No elements of discussion are offered; a simple statement of result is presented and it is the one most central to the aims of the study.

Sentence 12

The particular role that each of the variables plays in a learner's willingness to communicate is then revealed in sentence 12. Concerning the trait-like variable, the finding of the study is that it can determine an individual's general tendency. However, the second part of the sentence explains what the study found about the role of the second variable (its potential for predicting the decision that a learner might make about initiating communication within a particular context). So, we can see that the findings of the most central issue/question of the study have been presented before the findings of the subsidiary or additional issues/questions.

Sentence 13

This sentence simply extends the finding about the situational variable, namely, that it can change over time. What this actually means is unclear at this stage. However, sentence 14 extends our understanding of what may bring about change in different situations.

Sentence 14

The last of the key findings to be introduced to the reader is provided in sentence 14. Explaining that behavioural change can come about as a result of learners communicating in different classroom contexts, this sentence identifies six factors that may influence such behaviour. They are simply listed in the abstract because there is no space to provide additional detail. As you will see later, the Discussion of Results chapter of the thesis provides this elaboration. It discusses whether or not and the extent to which there may be particular patterns associated with their interaction.

Conclusion

Sentence 15

In the first of two concluding statements, sentence 15 makes a broad statement about the significance of the findings. It explains that the WTC construct is dynamic. Without detailing the specifics of its dynamism, we can, nevertheless, understand quite easily from what has been presented in sentences 11 to 14 that individual factors and contexts may play a major role in the changing nature of a learner's behaviour. We are told that the findings offer something new to this field of investigation and that the study has been worthwhile.

Sentence 16

The abstract closes with a confirmation that there are practical applications from the findings of the study that can be made to language learning classrooms. However, the guidelines and suggestions offered by the author are not presented here. We will find them recorded in the concluding chapter of the thesis. The final sentence also states that further research could be undertaken but, again, no mention of specific areas is provided at this point. This is not necessarily a shortcoming because references to specific applications and future areas of research are usually very clearly signaled in the concluding chapter of a thesis.

Before drawing conclusions from this analysis for further application, we are now going to consider another abstract. Written by an Applied Linguistics Doctoral student, we will be thinking about whether there are similarities and/or differences between it and the Masters abstract we have just been considering.

ANALYSIS OF A DOCTORAL THESIS ABSTRACT

As you read the following abstract in Box 2e, think about the moves and sub-moves that the author has included and about whether there are similarities and/or differences between this abstract and the Masters abstract. I would suggest that you write your move and sub-move choices in column two of Box 2e before comparing them with the analysis given in Box 2f. In order to see the similarities and differences between the Masters and Doctoral abstracts, you may find it helpful to create a chart that compares their move structures. Having done that, read the analysis that follows on the similarities and differences between the two abstracts.

Box 2e Abstract text and move structure

I. Current approaches to second language instruction have called for an integration of message-focused and form-focused instruction in the L2 classroom. 2. One way this may be accomplished is through incidental focus on form which draws learners' attention to linguistic items as they arise in meaning-focused interaction. 3. While incidental focus on form

---

Box 2e   (Continued)

has been theorized to benefit learners, little empirical research has investigated its actual effectiveness.

4. This study examined the occurrence and nature of incidental focus on form and its effectiveness in promoting L2 learning. 5. Thirty-two hours of naturally-occurring meaning-focused L2 lessons were observed in 12 different classes of young adults in a private language school. 6. Classroom interaction yielded 1,373 focus on form episodes (FFEs), occurring when there was a brief shift in attention from message to linguistic form. 7. These FFEs were transcribed and analysed for a variety of general characteristics and discourse moves. 8. A subset of 491 FFEs were used as a basis for individualized test items in which students who participated in specific FFEs were asked to recall the linguistic information provided in them.

9. The results showed that incidental focus on form did occur in these lessons, although the number of FFEs varied significantly among classes, teachers and students. 10. The FFEs were more frequently code-related and reactive in nature. 11. The response moves usually occurred immediately after the trigger, and generally provided linguistic information with a recast. 12. Uptake occurred in roughly three quarters of the FFEs, and it was generally successful. 13. Additionally, uptake was more likely to occur when the trigger was followed by an immediate elicitation response. 14. Successful uptake was also more likely to occur in FFEs targeting code-related student errors with immediate elicitation responses.

15. The results of the testing showed that learners were able to recall the targeted linguistic information correctly or partially correctly

nearly 60% of the time one day after the FFE, and 50% two weeks later. 16. Furthermore, successful uptake in an FFE was found to be a significant predictor of correct scores. 17. These results suggest that incidental focus on form may be of some benefit to learners, particularly if they are encouraged to incorporate the targeted linguistic items into their own production.

Box 2f Abstract text and move structure analysis

1. Current approaches to second language instruction have called for an integration of message-focused and form-focused instruction in the L2 classroom. 2. One way this may be accomplished is through incidental focus on form which draws learners' attention to linguistic items as they arise in meaning-focused interaction. 3. While incidental focus on form has been theorized to benefit learners, little empirical research has investigated its actual effectiveness.	Moves 1a, d (introduction – context, continue tradition) Move 1d (introduction – continue tradition) Moves 1c,d (introduction – importance, gap)
4. This study examined the occurrence and nature of incidental focus on form and its effectiveness in promoting L2 learning. 5. Thirty-two hours of naturally-occurring meaning-focused L2 lessons were observed in 12 different classes of young adults in a private language school. 6. Classroom interaction yielded 1,373 focus on form episodes (FFEs), occurring when there was a brief shift in attention from message to linguistic form. 7. These FFEs were transcribed and analysed for a variety of general characteristics and discourse moves. 8. A subset of 491 FFEs were used as a basis for individualized test items in which students who participated in specific FFEs were asked to recall the linguistic information provided in them.	Move 2a (purpose) Move 3b (method – design) Moves 3b,c (method – design, data source) Move 3d (method – analysis) Move 3d (method – analysis)

25

Box 2f   (Continued)

9. The results showed that incidental focus on form did occur in these lessons, although the number of FFEs varied significantly among classes, teachers and students. 10. The FFEs were more frequently code-related and reactive in nature. 11. The response moves usually occurred immediately after the trigger, and generally provided linguistic information with a recast. 12. Uptake occurred in roughly three quarters of the FFEs, and it was generally successful. 13. Additionally, uptake was more likely to occur when the trigger was followed by an immediate elicitation response. 14. Successful uptake was also more likely to occur in FFEs targeting code-related student errors with immediate elicitation responses.	Move 4a (product – finding 1) Move 4a (product – finding 1) Move 4a (product – finding 1) Move 4a (product – finding 1) Move 4a (product – finding 1) Move 4a (product – finding 1)
15. The results of the testing showed that learners were able to recall the targeted linguistic information correctly or partially correctly nearly 60% of the time one day after the FFE, and 50% two weeks later. 16. Furthermore, successful uptake in an FFE was found to be a significant predictor of correct scores. 17. These results suggest that incidental focus on form may be of some benefit to learners, particularly if they are encouraged to incorporate the targeted linguistic items into their own production.	Move 4a (product – finding 2) Move 4a (product – finding 2) Move 5a (conclusion – significance)

Glossary of terms used in the abstract

1. **message-focused instruction:** classroom teaching that focuses on the communication of meaning
2. **form-focused instruction:** classroom teaching that focuses on linguistic accuracy (e.g. grammar)

3. **incidental focus on form:** the unplanned, incidental provision of instruction on a linguistic form or structure (e.g. a grammar point)
4. **focus on form episode:** a unit of discourse/interaction between learners where the focus is on a linguistic point
5. **the trigger:** a statement that gives rise to another statement
6. **uptake:** accurate and appropriate use of a linguistic form or structure after it had been focused on

Similarities between the two abstracts

As well as providing an abstract of similar length to that of the first abstract, I think you can see here that there are other similarities between the two abstracts. Both include the same five moves. Broadly speaking, the strategies employed in the creation of these moves are similar even though some differences are evident.

Differences between the two abstracts

Moves within a sentence

The first difference between the abstracts concerns the inclusion of more than one move within a single sentence. This pattern characterizes a number of sentences in the first abstract but it does not occur at all in the second abstract. While links between moves are clearly and explicitly signaled when two moves appear within a single sentence, it does not necessarily mean that links are not made when this does not occur. Sentential links can be clearly and explicitly made between moves by other cohesive means. In comparing only one Masters and one Doctoral thesis, we could easily assume that these are differences that reflect the two types of thesis. However, this is not the case. It is rather a difference in individual style and preference. Any thesis needs to establish links between moves and between sentential propositions. The extent to which one approach is adopted more than another may be a feature of particular disciplines but generally it is the result of the writer's communicative style.

Introduction

Secondly, the Introduction move is slightly longer in the second abstract than it is in the first. This may have occurred because the author wanted to explain not only the context and importance of the topic in some detail and the need for further research in the area but also what is meant by the key term 'incidental focus on form'. The importance of defining and backgrounding this particular approach to form-focused instruction in some detail arises from the confusion that could result for those not familiar with different approaches to form-focused instruction. For example, the second language acquisition literature makes a significant distinction between two types of form-focused instructions but the difference is only signaled by a change in the use of one letter – either a capital 'S' (focus on formS) or a lower case 's' (focus on forms). Additionally, the second abstract seems to emphasize the limited amount of empirical research on the effectiveness of incidental focus on form, whereas this focus is less explicit in the first abstract. Again, the difference is not really one that distinguishes a Masters from a Doctoral thesis. Rather, it should be seen as a difference between the focus that two authors wish to provide or between two areas of investigation where the background of one needs more explanation than that of the other.

Purpose

A third difference is revealed in the more extensive statement of purpose provided in the first one. Whereas the second abstract referred to three purposes or aims within a single sentence, the first abstract identified each purpose or aim across four sentences and, in doing so, provided us with a more comprehensive and perhaps clearer understanding of the various aims of the study. The three key words in the purpose statement of the second abstract ('occurrence', 'nature' and 'effectiveness') become clear as we consider the Method and Product moves later in the abstract. It is possible that the author of the second abstract may have assumed that we would be more familiar with this field of investigation so confined himself to a single sentence.

Methodology

Fourthly, while similar detail on the methodology of each study is presented in the two abstracts, the second abstract devotes only four sentences to it, compared with the seven sentences provided in the first abstract. It is possible that fewer design features were specified by this author because of the single data source. By comparison, data for the first study, outlined in the first abstract, were sourced in several ways and these needed to be outlined in the abstract so that we would know how reliable and valid the findings of the study are. The approach to data analysis is not outlined in the first abstract but is described in detail in the methodology chapter of the thesis. It is likely that the author chose to refer to how the data were analyzed because of the relative novelty of the approach.

Product

The Purpose move of the second abstract, in sentence 4, revealed the following two primary foci of the research: (1) the occurrence and nature of incidental focus on form and (2) its effectiveness in promoting second language learning. The Product move is therefore presented in two parts as follows: (1) sentences 9–14 outline the first key finding and its associated findings and (2) sentences 15–16 refer to the second key finding. Compared with the Product move of the first abstract, similar detail on the findings of the second study is presented in the Product move of the second abstract.

Conclusion

Compared with the detail presented for the Method and Product moves of the two abstracts, less attention is given in both abstracts to the Conclusion move. In both cases, the significance of the research is mentioned, particularly its application possibilities.

Summary

In summary, we have seen that the same five moves and similar submoves were employed in both abstracts and that a similar amount of attention was given to each in the two abstracts. This is not surprising because both abstracts are introducing empirical research in the same discipline.

A KEY LINGUISTIC FEATURE OF A THESIS ABSTRACT

Tense

Arguably, one of the most important linguistic features to note when writing an abstract is the use of the appropriate tense. Because an abstract is reporting what has been done in the study that is about to be reported on, is contextualizing the study in the existing literature and/or is commenting on the extent of the study's contribution to that context, different verb tenses are required to convey these various details. Box 2g below identifies one example from the abstract of our sample Masters thesis to illustrate the usage of four different tenses. It should also be noted though that there may be some choice in the use of tense on some occasions. For example, in sentence 16, although the author has used the past simple tense to convey the point that practical implications and future research suggestions were identified, other authors may have chosen to use the present tense. In this situation, the choice will depend upon how the author views the writing of the abstract. For example, if it is seen as a description of the thesis itself (the document that the abstract is summarizing), it is appropriate to use the present tense. However, if the author views the abstract as a summary of the research that is reported in that document, the past simple tense will be appropriate.

Box 2g   Tense usage in thesis abstracts

Sentence	Tense	Example	Purpose
I	Present continuous	WTC...*is* currently *receiving* an increasing amount of attention...	To reveal ongoing work in this field of enquiry

2	Present perfect	The present study *has continued* that focus ...	To show that the present study was continuing a tradition by extending the research focus and that it has been completed
3	Past simple	MacIntyre et al. (1998) who *posited* that WTC ...	To report a completed action in the present study
15	Present simple	The results of this study *contribute* to an understanding ...	To explain the generalizability of the results of the study

FREQUENTLY ASKED QUESTIONS

1. How long should the abstract be?

There is no required length but most thesis abstracts are confined to 350–500 words.

2. When is it best to write the abstract?

The abstract is often the last part of the thesis to be written. However, some students may write a draft of the abstract at an earlier stage and refine it once the other parts of the thesis have been written.

3. How much detail is expected for each of the key moves of the abstract?

This will vary from thesis to thesis and from individual to individual. You will have noticed in our analysis of the two theses in this chapter how the Doctoral thesis provided more detail on the method and product moves than the Masters thesis did. Because the scope of the Doctoral thesis is greater, it is not uncommon for a thesis at this level to provide more detail on these moves. If your thesis is exploring new territory, it might be appropriate for you to provide more introductory and purpose sub-moves. Your supervisor will be able to guide you if you feel uncertain about what might be best in your case.

4. Should all the results be presented in the abstract?

The key results of your study should be presented in the abstract. You might also choose to include one or two of the more interesting subsidiary results. Certainly, you should include at least the main result for each of the research questions/hypotheses you investigated.

5. How specific should I be when referring to implications and applications of the study?

Again, this is an individual matter. Some authors will refer to the key areas of practice that might benefit from the results of the study and to one or two areas for further research. These are areas that often receive less attention in the abstract than other areas.

FURTHER ACTIVITIES

The following activities could be done individually, in pairs (with another thesis student or with your supervisor) or in small groups:

1. Select a journal article in your area of research interest, remove the abstract and read the full article. Imagine that what you have read is a shortened account of a full thesis. Drawing upon what you have learned while reading this chapter, write an abstract that would be suitable as a thesis abstract for the content you have read. Once you have completed the abstract, compare it with the one that you removed from the journal article. It will be interesting for you to compare the extent to which the various moves and sub-moves differ between the two.

2. By the time you read this book, you may have read a number of theses. If this is the case, select two or three and compare the move structure of each of their abstracts. If you have not read other theses, you could still do this activity. You may find in your university library some theses in your discipline area that could be used for this activity. Think about why any differences might have occurred and about any ways in which you think you

could improve the abstracts. You could compare the abstracts for Masters level theses, Doctoral level theses and Masters and Doctoral level theses.

3. If you have written a draft of your abstract, you could refer to the move and sub-move options presented earlier in this chapter to evaluate what you have written.

FURTHER READING

If you are interested in reading some of the literature that has informed the material presented in this chapter, you may find the following references useful:

Cooley, L., & Lewkowicz, J. (2003). *Dissertation Writing in Practice: Turning Ideas into Text*. Hong Kong: Hong Kong University Press.

Hyland, K. (2000). Speaking as an insider: Promotion and credibility in abstracts. In K. Hyland, *Disciplinary Discourses: Social Interactions in Academic Writing* (pp. 63–84). London: Longman.

Kaplan, R., Cantor, S., Hagstrom, C., Lia, D., Shiotani, Y., & Zimmerman, C. (1994). On abstract writing. *Text, 14*, 401–426.

Paltridge, B., & Starfield, S. (2007). *Thesis and Dissertation Writing in a Second Language: A Handbook for Supervisors*. New York: Routledge.

Rudestam, K., & Newton, R. (2001). *Surviving your Dissertation: A Comprehensive Guide to Content and Process*. Newbury Park, CA: Sage.

Salager-Mayer, F. (1990). Discoursal flaws in medical English abstracts: A genre analysis per research and text type. *Text, 10*, 365–384.

Swales, J. (1990). *Genre Analysis: English in Academic and Research Settings*. Cambridge: Cambridge University Press.

3 Introduction

INTRODUCTION

In this chapter, we will be considering the opening chapter of a thesis. First, we will reflect on its purpose or functions and then look at the type of content that is typically presented and at ways in which it might be organized. Having considered these options, we will then analyze the extent to which the introductory chapter of our sample Masters thesis used these options. This analysis will lead on to a discussion of some of the linguistic features that are characteristic of introductory chapters. Before concluding the chapter, we will look at some frequently asked questions, suggest some with follow-up activities and provide a list of references for further reading.

THE FUNCTIONS OF A THESIS INTRODUCTION

The primary purpose of the introductory chapter is to acquaint the reader to the thesis. Most often, this will involve a consideration of the steps presented below in Box 3a.

Box 3a   Functions of a thesis introduction

1. A description of the problem, issue or question that interests you
2. A review of the background and context of the study, including a review of what is known from the available literature about the area you are interested in
3. An identification of gaps in this body of knowledge
4. An explanation of what you plan to do to address one or more of these gaps

---

5. An outline of how you plan to carry out your investigation, together with an indication of the scope and delimitations of your study
6. An explanation of what you believe your contribution will be to this area of knowledge
7. An outline of the content and structure of your thesis

Although it is not essential that you cover all of these steps, you should at least consider each one and have a considered reason for not including any of them. In the following section, we will look in more detail at how these functions might be achieved in the opening chapter.

THE CONTENT AND STRUCTURE OF A THESIS INTRODUCTION

As we have seen in Chapter 1 of this book, researchers, over the years, have analyzed the typical content and organizational patterns of different parts of a thesis and produced frameworks of what they have found. When you read the list of references at the end of this chapter, you will see that quite a lot of attention has been given to the introductory chapter of theses and the corresponding section of research articles. The material presented in this chapter draws upon these analyses and has been summarized in Box 3b below.

Box 3b Introduction move and sub-move options

Moves	Sub-moves
I. Establish a research territory	a. Explain the extent to which it is important, central, interesting, problematic or relevant
	b. Provide background information about the area
	c. Introduce (and review) aspects of previous research in the area
	d. Define terms and constructs

Box 3b   (Continued)

Moves	Sub-moves
2. Establish a niche	a. Indicate a gap in previous research b. Raise a question about previous research c. Identify a problem or need d. Extend previous knowledge
3. Occupy the niche	a. Outline purpose, aim and objectives of present research b. Specify the research questions/hypotheses that were investigated c. Outline the theoretical perspectives/positions d. Describe the methodology and design of the research e. Indicate the scope/delimitations of the research f. Explain the contribution and value of the research to the field of knowledge g. outline the chapter organization of the thesis

---

As you can see, the first column outlines the key areas of content (main moves) and the second column outlines a range of sub-moves that might be considered for developing each main move. You will note that these are presented as options rather than requirements. In the analysis of our sample introductory chapter, we will see the extent to which the author has utilized each of these moves. Then, when you analyze the move structure of the Doctoral introductory chapter in the activities section of this chapter, you will be able to see a number of ways in which the two chapters are different and, in doing so, see that each approach is equally valid and effective in terms of introducing the reader to the thesis.

ANALYSIS OF A MASTERS THESIS INTRODUCTION

In this section, we will analyze and discuss the moves used by the author of our Masters introductory chapter. As I suggested in the previous chapter, when discussing the content and structure of the thesis abstract, I would suggest that you use the main and sub moves presented in Box 3b above to try to identify which options have been used in the chapter before you look at the analysis provided. You will need to cover the right hand side of the text with a sheet of paper.

If you have browsed through the chapter of this book before reading the chapters more closely, you would have noticed that, unlike the chapters following this one, the author has not provided an introductory section to outline the content of her chapter. The introductory chapter of some theses does include this kind of advance organizer but it is more typical for one to not to be provided with the opening chapter. However, the choice is yours.

Section 1.1 Background of the study

In this section, we focus our attention on the first of three sections – the background informing the focus of the study.

Box 3c   Section 1.1 – Background of the study

1. For many learners, the ultimate goal of language learning is to use the language for authentic and effective communication in everyday life. 2. This conforms to the concept of communicative language teaching (CLT), a dominant feature of modern language pedagogy, which places its major emphasis on learning through communication (Ellis 2004). 3. Long's (1996) update of the Interaction Hypothesis has suggested that second language interaction provides learners with opportunities to receive comprehensible input, to produce and modify their output, to test out hypotheses and to notice gaps existing in their interlanguage, which in turn, can facilitate language development (Mackey 2002: 380).

Move 1b
(background)

4. It has been argued by some researchers (for example, Skehan 1989) that language is best learnt through communication, a notion stressing that 'learners have to talk in order to learn' (Skehan 1989: 48). 5. Swain's (1985,

---

Box 3c (Continued)

1995) Output Hypothesis suggested that output serves as oral practice by providing opportunities for learners to test hypotheses about the rules they have constructed for the target language. 6. At the same time, this may lead to greater meta-linguistic awareness so that learners may pay particular attention to form. 7. This may in turn cause them to 'notice a gap between what they want to say and what they can say, leading them to recognize what they do not know, or know only partially' (Swain 1995: 125, 126) in the process of struggling to produce output comprehensible to their interlocutors (Mackey 2002).

8. In the last decade, there has been a growing body of research that has had as its focus, an individual difference variable – willingness to communicate (WTC) – a non-linguistic construct that would seem to be of obvious interest in the area of communicative language teaching (Ellis 2004). 9. Some researchers – for example, MacIntyre, Clément, Dörnyei and Noels 1998; MacIntyre, Baker, Clément and Donovan 2003 – have advocated that a fundamental goal of second language education should be the creation of willingness to communicate in the language learning process, in order to produce students who are willing to seek out communication opportunities and to use the language for authentic communication. 10. MacIntyre, Baker, Clément and Conrod (2001) have argued that WTC should be expected to facilitate the language learning process, a view based on their finding that higher WTC among students translates into increased opportunity for practice in an L2 and authentic L2 usage.

Moves 1a,b,c (centrality, background, previous research)

11. A widely accepted definition of WTC in L2 was suggested by MacIntyre et al. (1998: 547), who considered this construct as 'a readiness to enter into discourse at a particular time with a specific person or persons, using an L2'. 12. Specific to an L2 classroom, WTC was defined by Oxford (1997: 449) as 'a student's intention to interact with others in the target language, given a chance to do so'. 13. Both definitions emphasized that

Move 1d (definitions)

one would have the freedom to decide whether to communicate or not in a particular context. 14. Also, both
definitions treated WTC in a very broad sense, which
included its applications to both written and spoken communication. 15. In their study, MacIntyre et al. (2001)
examined WTC in four macro skills of speaking, listening,
reading and writing, both inside and outside the classroom.
16. Given the scope of this present study, WTC will be
considered only in terms of spoken communication and
within an L2 classroom.

Move 1c
(previous
research)
Move 3e
(scope)

As you look at the move analysis in column two, you will see that
this first section is primarily made up of move 1 content in order
to introduce us to the research territory the author has conducted
her research in. The only deviation from this occurs in the last sentence where move 3 has been included. This move is likely to have
been included so that we can understand at the outset that she has
focused her research on one particular area of the wider research
territory that has just been outlined.

Paragraphs 1–2

In the first seven sentences, background information about the
wider research territory is provided. Essentially, these sentences
are introducing us to the theoretical framework that she is working within. We are introduced to what key theorists have to say
about the aim of second language learning and how they believe it
occurs. It is within this context that the specific theoretical focus of
her research is placed: the contribution of one variable (a learner's
willingness to communicate in a language learning classroom) to
the learning process.

Paragraph 3

These sentences of paragraph three, introduce us (1) to the
centrality and importance of the specific area of research within
the wider context (*move 1a*); (2) to the theoretical belief that a
willingness to communicate is an essential part of the language

learning process (*move 1b*) and (3) to one piece of empirical research that supports the relationship between a willingness to communicate and the taking of opportunities to communicate in the second language (*move 1c*).

Paragraph 4

In these four sentences, the willingness to communicate construct is defined. A broad definition is provided in sentence 11 before a specific definition related to second language classrooms is given in sentence 12. Sentences 13 and 14 then explain how both definitions include the freedom that individuals have about whether or not they will communicate and how both relate to written and spoken communication. The focus of one earlier study on willingness to communicate in four macro skills (move 1c) is then introduced (sentence 15). The final sentence in this section announces the scope of the study (move 3e) to be reported in the following chapters of the thesis – an investigation of a learner's willingness to communicate orally. Thus, the scope and delimitations of the thesis have been announced as a lead-in to the following section on the specific aims of the research.

Overview of move characteristics in this section

Several noteworthy move characteristics are evident in this first section of the introduction:

1. Apart from the last sentence where move 3e provides a lead-in to the following section, Section 1.1 comprises only move 1. There is nothing surprising about this as we should expect the opening section to introduce us to the wider context and motivation for the study.
2. All four sub-moves a–d, outlined in the options of Box 3b above, have been included in this section, so the territory that the author was working in has been fully established.
3. Some of the sub-moves have been recycled (1b and 1c) and there is no strict ordering of these from 1a to 1d. As sub-move

options, there is no prescribed order in which they should appear or frequency with which they may be included.

Section 1.2 Aims of the research

Before reading the text in Box 3d on the second section of the introduction, you may like to cover up column two with a sheet of paper and, using the information provided in Box 3b on move and submove options, do your own analysis of the move structure as you read the text.

Box 3d   Section1.2 – Aims of the research

17. The primary purpose of the study is to explore the dual characteristics of the willingness to communicate construct, following the trait/state dichotomy claimed by some researchers; that is, it aims to examine whether the willingness to communicate construct operates at the trait level or at the state level. 18. The study also aims to investigate how the construct operates in three interactional contexts in a second language classroom: whole class, small groups and dyads.

Move 3a
(aims)

19. The study involved eight international students enrolled in a general English program at a language school in Auckland. 20. Their self-report WTC was identified by means of a WTC questionnaire at the beginning of the program. 21. Then, during the entire span of the program, the learners' WTC behavior in a whole class situation was observed and recorded on a classroom observation scheme. 22. WTC behavior in groups and dyads was also examined in terms of the students' task performance in group and pair work, which was audio-taped and coded on the classroom observation scheme subsequently. 23. Factors that learners perceived as being most important in determining their WTC in class were explored through interviews with volunteer participants.

Move 3d,e
(method, scope)

Box 3d   (Continued)

24. In general, the current study has employed a multiple research approach in order to provide a more holistic and comprehensive view of the WTC construct in second language learning.

Move 3d
(method)

25. This study contributes to an understanding of the role played by WTC in second language instruction, through an exploration of how WTC operates in a second language classroom. 26. While a number of studies related to the present research have been undertaken in the past (see MacIntyre et al. 2001, 2003; Yashima et al. 2002, 2004), the focus of this earlier work was based predominantly on self-report, rather than actual classroom behavior. 27. Arguably, there remains a need to incorporate a qualitative approach to examine WTC, in order to verify antecedents affecting WTC through behavioral studies of the L2 classroom. 28. The dynamic aspect of WTC – that is to say, how WTC varies over time – was largely ignored in previous studies. 29. This present study differs from these to the extent that it provides more comprehensive evidence covering both WTC based on a self-report questionnaire and WTC in actual behavior, as well as the dynamics of the WTC construct. 30. The results of this study may therefore be of benefit in second language instruction if they convince instructors of the importance of creating WTC among learners in the L2 classroom.

Move 3f
(contribution)

Move 2a (gap)

Move 2c
(need)

Move 2a
(gap)

Moves 3a,f
(aim,
contribution)

Move 3f
(contribution)

Paragraph 1

This section of the introduction chapter begins with an announcement of the two key aims of the study. You will notice that the author has not explicitly presented a move 2 in order to establish the niche or gap in the field of research. Most often, authors will include a move 2 before introducing move 3. However, in this case, it could be argued that the author has indirectly established a niche with her reference in sentence 17 to the claim by some researchers that a trait/state dichotomy exists and that, by implication, it needs to be investigated and resolved. Later in this section, you will see that a more explicit announcement of the niche/gap is provided.

Paragraph 2

Having announced the aims of the research, the author proceeds to explain its scope or delimitations (*move 3e*) and describes some key elements of the methodology that were employed (*move 3d*). Sentence 19 explains that only eight international students took part in the study and that they were enrolled in a general English programme at a language school in Auckland, New Zealand. Then, in sentences 20–23, we read about the specific methods that were used to collect the research data: questionnaire (sentence 20), observation scheme and audio-taping (sentences 21 and 22) and interviews (sentence 23).

Paragraph 3

In a stand-alone sentence, move 3d continues with a statement about the overall methodological approach of the study (multi-method) and a justification for this particular approach (to provide a more holistic and comprehensive view of the willingness to communicate construct). Some authors might consider placing their statement about the overall methodology before their outline of the specific methods they used for collecting their data.

Paragraph 4

In the final paragraph of this section, the student explains the aim of her research (*move 3a*) and what she considers to be its contribution to the wider field of knowledge (*move 3f*) and, in doing so, relates it to several statements about the need for the investigation (*moves 2a and 2c*). In sentence 25, she explains that the study contributes to the understanding we already have of the role played by a learner's willingness to contribute in the second language learning process. In particular, she states that her unique contribution to this area of investigation lies in her investigation of it in a second language classroom environment. In sentence 26, she explains that research has previously been undertaken but that it was primarily concerned with investigating what learners said about their willingness to communicate rather than with a more objective investigation that examined the relationship between what they say and what they actually do in the classroom. Thus, her contribution to the field has been to carry out a study that combines both approaches (sentence 27). A second gap in the existing research (*move 2a*) is stated in sentence 28. Having identified areas in which further research is needed, the student proceeds to state how her research has filled that gap or need (*moves 3a and 3f*). In sentence 30, she concludes this section of the chapter with a specific statement of how the findings from the study could be applied in the second language classroom (*move 3f*).

Overview of move characteristics in this section

Similarly, we can note a number of characteristics about the way in which this section of the introduction has been structured:

1. Unlike many theses, where move 2 precedes move 3, this section introduces us to the aims of the study before the research gap or niche is explicitly stated. However, one could possibly argue that the author has indirectly established the niche or gap to be occupied in sentences 8–10.
2. Explicit references to the niche or gap are integrated into the move 3 sub-moves in sentences 25–30. As such, they have been introduced in the context of how previous research will be developed as a result of the focus of this study.
3. As we saw in the first section, the recycling of sub-moves also occurs in this section. Sub-moves 3d and 3e follow quite logically and coherently from sub-move 3a at the beginning of this section.

Section 1.3 Organization of the study

This section of the chapter provides an overview of how the remaining chapters of the thesis have been organized. In many respects, it is like an expanded version of a table of contents. The relationship between chapters is made clear as the author outlines some of the main content areas of each chapter and, in doing so, introduces us to the 'argument' of the thesis. In a sense, the paragraph structure of this section follows the structural outline of the abstract. In short, it tells the reader *how* the thesis is organized and, to some extent, *why* it is done in this way.

Box 3e   Section 1.3 – Organization of the study

31. This thesis consists of six chapters. 32. Following this introduction, Chapter 2 reviews extant literature and research that motivates and generates the research questions addressed in this thesis. 33. It also considers, from a variety of perspectives, how WTC research represents a new trend in motivational research, and reviews some major findings from empirical research studies concerning WTC in both L1 and L2. 34. Gaps in previous research are subsequently identified and the research questions are raised for investigation. | Move 3g (thesis outline)

35. Chapter 3 depicts the methodological approach adopted in the study. 36. In order to enrich the data from different perspectives, a multi-method design was adopted; justification for this approach is provided. 37. It is contended that such a research design is advantageous to the extent that it offers the possibility of providing results that complement, elaborate and confirm each other. 38. The major research instruments – the Willingness to Communicate Survey, a classroom observation scheme, and structured interviews, are identified and the procedures followed in collecting and analyzing data are stated.

39. Key findings from an analysis of the research data are presented in Chapter 4. 40. These include results based on the use of both qualitative and quantitative research techniques. 41. Results from a content analysis of the interview data are also considered.

Box 3e   (Continued)

42. Chapter 5 includes a detailed account and interpretation of the findings of the study, with reference to each of the research questions and in relation to previous relevant research findings.

43. Chapter 6 summarizes the study findings, focuses on both pedagogical and research implications of the study, and indicates its limitations.

Paragraph 1

Sentence 31 states that the thesis is made up of 6 chapters. Sentences 32–34 explain that Chapter 2, following this introductory chapter, provides a literature review of the wider field in which the specific focus of the research is situated. Thus, it introduces us to the motivation of the research and to the research questions of the study (sentence 32). Sentence 33 then explains that Chapter 2 will consider the importance and significance of the study, together with a review of the published research literature on the willingness to communicate construct in both first and second language contexts. Finally, sentence 34 states that Chapter 2 will conclude with a statement on where gaps in previous research lie and an announcement on which of these, stated as research questions, were investigated in the study. Thus, we are told that Chapter 2 will introduce us to (1) the literature informing the study, (2) the motivation for the research, (3) the specific focus of the study (research questions), (4) the importance/significance of the research focus, (5) the available research findings, (6) the gaps in this research base and (7) how these gaps were addressed in the study.

Paragraph 2

The methodological approach of the thesis, outlined in Chapter 3, is outlined in sentences 35–38. We are told that the overall approach will be explained (sentence 35). In the following sentence, we are told that the multi-method design that was chosen will be justified, together with the advantages of employing such an approach (sentence 37). We then learn in sentence 38 that this chapter will outline the specific data collection methods and the procedures that were adopted for the collection and analysis of the data. Thus, we are told that Chapter 3 will introduce us to (1) the methodology, (2) a justification for the approach including its advantages, (3) the data collection methods and (4) how the data were collected and analyzed.

Paragraph 3

Next, we learn that Chapter 4 will present the findings of the study (sentence 39). Sentence 40 then explains that both qualitative and quantitative findings will be provided. We could debate whether it was then necessary to explain in sentence 41 that a content analysis of the interview data is included in the chapter. Why one aspect of the qualitative findings has been singled out for specific mention is not clear. The author probably had a very good reason for doing this. In writing this part of the chapter, you need to make a number of judgement calls on what level of detail to include and what not to include. You should ask your supervisor to guide you in these decisions. In this paragraph, then, we have been told that the methodology chapter will present us with the findings of the study and that they will be presented in several sections.

Paragraph 4

In a stand-alone sentence, we are told that Chapter 5 will discuss the findings of the study and that they will be discussed in relation to each of the research questions and in relation to the wider research presented in Chapter 2. Thus, we learn that this chapter will be concerned with (1) discussing the research findings of the study, (2) using the findings to answer the research questions and (3) discussing their significance and contribution to the big picture presented in Chapter 2.

Paragraph 5

This introductory chapter concludes with an outline of what is discussed in the final chapter of the thesis: (1) a summary of the study's findings, (2) the pedagogical and research implications of the study and (3) the limitations of the study. When you have read Chapter 8 of this book on the conclusion chapter, you may want to reflect on whether this outline includes all the areas that were presented. Also, you might want to think about the positioning of the acknowledgement of any limitations of your study. Here, the student has placed hers after her discussion of the implications of the study. It may be more appropriate to discuss limitations after the findings have been summarized so that any caveats are considered before recommendations are made about how the findings could be applied. Additionally, it might also be more logical to discuss future research ideas after your discussion of limitations. These are issues that you should discuss with your supervisor.

Overview of move characteristics in this section

The most obvious feature of this final section is its focus on move 3g. The previous two sections have introduced us to the context in which the study was situated, the aims of the study and the contribution that the research is expected to make to wider field of knowledge, so all that remains is for the reader to be introduced to the way in which the study will be reported in the thesis.

SOME KEY LINGUISTICS FEATURES OF A THESIS INTRODUCTION

There are a number of linguistic features that are worth highlighting about the writing of a thesis introduction. While they are characteristic of this chapter, they are also features that you need to be aware of when writing the other chapters of your thesis. Because we are focusing our attention on them here for the first time, our discussion will be more extensive than that provided in other chapters of the book. First, we will look at the choice of verb tense and voice because appropriateness can vary a lot within even a short piece of discourse. Then we will consider certain vocabulary choices like the use of adjectives, first person pronouns, contrastive vocabulary and structures and meta-text or meta-discourse.

Tense

As you will see, certain tense options should be considered for the three main moves.

Move 1 (establishing a research territory)

When describing the importance or centrality of the problem, issue or question that your study focused on, you should make use of the *present tense* and the *present perfect tense*. The *present tense* will be used to describe the present situation and to convey the idea that the point being made is a generally accepted truth. In sentence 1 below, from our sample introduction, we can see, for example, that the present tense 'is' has been used to inform us that the ultimate goal of language learning is to use it for communication in everyday life. Thus, it is presented as a statement of truth for many learners and as one that is therefore presently the case.

> For many learners, the ultimate goal of language learning *is* to use the language for authentic and effective communication in everyday life. (sentence 1)

The *present perfect tense* is used to refer to what has happened up to the present point in time. In sentence 8 below from our sample introduction, we can see that the growing body of research being introduced is something that has been occurring up to the present day.

> In the last decade, there *has been* a growing body of research that *has had* as its focus, an individual variable.... (sentence 8)

As you then describe theoretical perspectives and research that has taken place in the field, you will be making use of both the *present perfect tense* and the *past simple tense*. If you are describing what has been done in this area of research up to and including the present day, you will use the *present perfect tense*. This can be seen, for example, in sentence 9 of our sample introduction where the

49

author is referring to a view that has been advanced by a number of researchers over time (including the present day):

> Some researchers – for example, MacIntyre, Clement, Dornyei and Noels 1998; MacIntyre, Baker, Clement and Donovan 2003 – *have advocated* that a fundamental goal of second language education should be the creation of willingness to communicate…. (sentence 9)

In the following sentence, you can see that the *past simple tense* has been used because the author is referring to a study that has been completed:

> In their study, MacIntyre et al. (2001) *examined* WTC in four macro skills of speaking, listening, reading and writing, both inside and outside the classroom. (sentence 15)

Move 2 (establishing a niche)

When it comes to identifying a niche or gap in the available research, you will be likely to use the *present perfect tense* and/or the *present simple tense*. You can see, for example, in sentence 26 of our sample text, that the *present perfect tense* has been used to describe what has not been investigated up to the present point in time.

> While a number of studies related to the present research *have been undertaken* in the past (see MacIntyre et al., 2001, 2003; Yashima et al. 2002, 2004), the focus of this earlier work *was based* predominantly on self-report, rather than actual classroom behavior. (sentence 26)

Move 3 (occupying the niche)

As you explain how your research sought to occupy the research niche, you will want to explain what the aims of your investigation were. If you are explaining your aims as goals that have been achieved, you are most likely to use the *past simple tense*. However, if you are writing your introduction as statement on what has yet to be revealed in the thesis, you would be more likely to use the *present simple tense*. In our sample introduction, you can see that the author has chosen the latter option in sentences 17 and 18.

> The primary purpose of the study *is* to explore ....(sentence 17)

> The study also *aims* to investigate .... (sentence 18)

When other sub-moves of move 3 are presented, they are most often reported as completed actions and so, as we can see in sentence 19, the *past simple tense* is used because the author chose to use the active voice. However, in sentence 23, she has used the *present perfect tense*. As we will see in our discussion below, this has been done because of her use of the passive voice.

> The study *involved* eight international students ......(sentence 19)

> Factors that learners perceived as being most important in determining their WTC in class *were explored* through interviews with volunteer participants. (sentence 23)

It should be noted in sentences 25, 29 and 30, however, that in presenting sub-move 3f (explaining the expected contribution and value of the research to the field of knowledge), the *present simple tense* has been used because the author is claiming that her research contributes now to our further understanding of the research territory it is situated in.

> This study *contributes* .... (sentence 25)

> This present study *differs* from these .... (sentence 29)

> The results of this study may .... (sentence 30)

Active versus passive voice

You can see that both the active and passive voices have been included in our sample introduction. There is no hard and fast rule on this. It is a matter of whether or not you, as author, wish to give prominence at the beginning of a sentence to the object of the sentence rather than the subject. If this is the case, you will use the *present perfect tense* rather than the *present tense*. In some situations, if the author does not want to reveal the subject of a sentence (for whatever reason), s/he will tend to use the passive voice. On other occasions, authors may want to make a stronger statement or suggest that something is an established fact so they will make use of the passive voice. In our sample introduction, you can see, in the following sentences, that the author has made quite extensive use of the passive voice. In each case, it is likely that she wanted to give prominence to the object of the sentence.

> Gaps in previous research *are* subsequently *identified* and the research questions *are raised* for investigation. (sentence 34)

> Key findings from an analysis of the research data *are presented* in Chapter 4. (sentence 39)

In sentence 37, we can see that a very clear decision has been made to not mention who the contenders of this claim are.

> *It is contended* that such a research design is advantageous ......(sentence 37)

Adjectives

Adjectives are often included in sub-move 1a statements in order to emphasize the importance or centrality of the research territory and research focus of the study to be reported. You can see, for example, in sentence 2, through the use of the adjective 'dominant', that the focus on a communicative use of language in language learning classes (the wider research territory of the study) has been central to research in the field.

> This conforms to the concept of communicative language teaching (CLT), a *dominant* feature of modern language pedagogy ......(sentence 2)

Compared with other theses that often include adjectives like 'unique', 'important' or 'significant', this introductory chapter is more reserved in the way it frames the importance of the study's focus. The importance and significance of the research territory are nevertheless conveyed by other means – a series of clear and extensive contextual statements.

First person pronouns

Opinions vary about whether to use the first person pronouns 'I' and 'we' in academic texts like the thesis. Some disciplines/departments/schools or individual supervisors believe that the use of the first person is too personal for an objective piece of academic reporting. As we have seen above, one way of getting around the issue is to make use of the passive voice. We saw a number of examples of this in the final section of our sample introduction.

> Key findings from an analysis of the research data *are presented* in Chapter 4. (sentence 39)

The question of whether or not to use the first person pronoun will be one that you need to decide on especially when presenting meta-discourse or meta-text like we saw in move 3g above when the author was explaining to the reader how the following chapters of the thesis have been structured. The same decision needs to be made when summarizing or reviewing what has been presented in a previous section of the thesis. While the decision is really yours, it would be best to consult with your supervisor to see if your discipline or institution requires a particular convention.

Contrastive vocabulary and structures

When it comes to identifying the niche that your research occupies, several different approaches might be taken. One of the more common techniques used to signal a gap in the research territory is the use of contrasting conjunctions and phrases.

Another approach that is frequently used is to include negative words or phrases that in some way highlight the fact that while 'x' may have been examined, 'y' has not been investigated. In our sample introduction, we can see that the author has made this contrast in a couple of different ways. In the sentence 26, she uses the structure 'while ('x' has occurred), (y) has not'.

> *While* a number of studies related to the present research have been undertaken in the past..., the focus of this earlier work was based

predominantly on self-report, *rather than* actual classroom behavior. (sentence 26)

Sometimes, the gap or niche may be signaled in a very direct manner. In our sample introduction, this approach has been used in sentences 27 and 28.

Arguably, there *remains a need* to incorporate a qualitative approach......(sentence 27)

The dynamic aspect of WTC...*was largely ignored* in previous studies. (sentence 28)

If you read other theses, you will see that an almost endless range of lexical and structural approaches can be used to signal the research niche. Swales and Feak (2004) present examples of some of this range and, in doing so, point out the need to use them with care:

1. *Verbs*
   Disregard; fail to consider; ignore; is limited to; misinterpret; neglect to consider; overestimate; overlook; suffer from; underestimate
2. *Adjectives*
   Controversial; incomplete; inconclusive; misguided; questionable; unconvincing; unsatisfactory
3. *Noun phrases*
   Little information, attention, work, data, research
   Few studies, investigations, researchers, attempts
   No studies, data, calculations
   None of these studies, findings, calculations
4. *Passive forms*
   It remains clear that
   It would be of interest to

Meta-discourse/meta-text

Meta-text or meta-discourse is used quite extensively in a thesis. It is the means by which the author talks about his/her writing and how it is organized. In other words, it is discourse that guides us through the text we are reading. At times, it will point us forward (as we saw in sections 2 and 3 of our sample thesis where the author was explaining her research aims and the way in which the thesis has been organized) and at other times it will point us back to earlier content (as we will see in summaries and overviews of material that has already been presented). In doing this, a range of typical linguistic features can be drawn upon. In pointing us forward, the author might present the following sentence in an introductory statement, for example, about the focus of a new chapter, and, in doing so, make use of a wide range of verbs:

This chapter will investigate, describe, introduce, present, develop, discuss, argue, show, reveal, report, focus...

In pointing us back to earlier content, the sentence might be presented in the following way:

This chapter has investigated, described, introduced, presented, developed, discussed, argued, showed, revealed, reported, focused...

Examples for pointing the reader forward in the introduction of our sample thesis can be seen in Box 3d (where the author is explaining the aims of her study) and in Box 3e (where she is explaining how the thesis is structured).

You will note that, in pointing the reader forward, either the present tense or future tense is used, and, in pointing back, the past simple tense or the present perfect tense is used.

FREQUENTLY ASKED QUESTIONS

1. How long should the Introduction be?

This is a difficult question to answer because there can be such a lot of variation even within theses/dissertations of particular disciplines. If the introductory chapter is written as a separate chapter from the literature review chapter(s), it may be around 5–10 pages. The word count of the Introduction of our sample Masters thesis was approximately 12,500 words. Applied Linguistics introductions are often shorter than the Introductions of theses in other disciplines. This is often because their literature reviews are more extensive than those of other disciplines.

2. Should the Introduction include references to the published literature?

Key references informing the field of enquiry and the focus of a study, such as seminal works, are often presented in the introduction. However, extensive referencing is not the norm. The display of extensive literature knowledge occurs in the literature review chapter(s).

3. Should I write the Introduction before the other chapters?

Many supervisors encourage their students to write a first draft of the introduction quite early on in the thesis-writing process. Some even suggest that their students do this during the data collection phase of their study, once most of the literature has been reviewed. It is very much an individual matter. Often, the introduction will be redrafted a number of times, the final draft being completed after most of the other chapters have been written. This is because aspects of the study may be modified in some way during the writing up of the results and the discussion of the results chapters.

4. Are there any differences between the Introductions of Masters and Doctoral theses?

A Doctoral introduction may be longer than a Masters Introduction for the very reason that the scope of the study is greater. It may also be the case that the Doctoral design and methodology is more elaborate than that of a Masters study. There may be other reasons as well, for example, the range of areas that the literature (theoretical and contextual) informing the study draws upon is wider. However, in terms of the moves and sub-moves that are included in the chapter, there is unlikely to be any substantial difference between the two.

5. To what extent should terms and constructs be defined in the Introduction?

The first time that a reader meets a concept, term or construct, it needs to be glossed or defined. Most often, this specialized vocabulary is introduced in the introduction chapter. However, it is unlikely that all terminology will first be met in the introduction. More detailed terminology will usually be met in the literature review while aspects of the methodology and methods employed will usually not be introduced until they are first encountered in the methodology chapter.

FURTHER ACTIVITIES

The following activities could be done individually, in pairs (with another thesis student or with your supervisor) or in small groups:

1. Select two or three Masters or Doctoral theses in your field of interest and compare their sub-headings. Are there any differences? If so, why do you think they exist?
2. Using two of the theses you chose for activity one above, see if you can identify any similarities and differences in the move structure of their introductions. If you identify any differences, think about why this might be the case and list your reasons.
3. Referring to the introductions of the same theses you used for activity two, use the list of linguistic features above to identify the extent to which they have been employed.
4. If you have written a draft of your introduction chapter, you could refer to the move and sub-move options presented earlier in this chapter to evaluate what you have written.

FURTHER READING

If you are interested in reading some of the literature that has informed the material presented in this chapter, you may find the following references useful:

Bunton, D. (2002). Generic moves in PhD thesis introductions. In J. Flowerdew (Ed.), *Academic Discourse*. London: Longman.

Dudley-Evans, T. (1986). Genre analysis: An investigation of the introduction and discussion sections of MSc dissertations. In M. Coulthard (Ed.), *Talking About Text*. Birmingham, UK: University of Birmingham.

Evans, D., & Gruba, P. (2002). *How to Write a Better Thesis*. (pp. 57–67) Melbourne, Australia: Melbourne University Press.

Paltridge, B., & Starfield, S. (2007). *Thesis and Dissertation Writing in a Second language: A handbook for supervisors*. New York: Routledge.

Rudestam, K., & Newton, R. (2001). *Surviving Your Dissertation: A Comprehensive Guide to Content and Process*. Newbury Park, CA: Sage.

Swales, J. (1990). *Genre Analysis: English in Academic and Research Settings*. Cambridge: Cambridge University Press.

Swales, J., & Feak, C. (2004). *Academic Writing for Graduate Students*. Ann Arbor: University of Michigan Press.

4 Literature Review

INTRODUCTION

In this chapter, we will be considering the functions of the literature review chapter(s), how to go about deciding what content should be included and how to most effectively organize it. This is usually the first chapter to be attempted by students. Often the first draft is written during the preparation of a thesis proposal and then expanded before you finally decide on the various components of your methodology. Thereafter, sections of the literature review will be revised with new material being added and with some existing material possibly being excluded. This process may continue up to the point where you have finished discussing your findings. More will be said about the reasons for this when we come to the discussion of results chapter.

You may be reading this chapter without having read the earlier chapters because you want to know how to go about creating a literature review for your research proposal. Therefore, we will consider ways of creating the first draft of the review. In doing so, we will look at the body of the literature review before its introduction and conclusion. But, in order to understand what is involved in this process, we need to consider first the various aims or functions of the literature review chapter.

THE FUNCTIONS OF A THESIS LITERATURE REVIEW

Having introduced your reader to the issue, problem or question in the introduction chapter, the aim of the literature review is to provide an in-depth account of the background literature relevant to the context that your study is situated in and, in doing so, to provide an 'argument', 'case' or justification for the study. In order to do this, there are essentially seven key functions that you should consider. These are presented in Box 4a below.

Box 4a   Functions of a thesis literature review

1. A review of the **non-research literature** that summarizes and synthesizes background and contextual information
2. A review of **theoretical perspectives** that underpin or inform your research project
3. A review of the **research literature** relevant to your study
4. A **critique** that

   (a) identifies arguments for and against issues and controversies related to functions 1–3 above and
   (b) assesses or weighs up the value of theories, ideas, claims, research designs, methods and conclusions, including an identification of strengths and weaknesses.

5. An identification of **gaps or shortcomings** in this knowledge and research
6. A **rationale** justifying why the gap was important and significant enough to be filled
7. An explanation of **how the design and execution of your research project was informed** by steps 1–6 above. This is likely to explain how the literature provided

   (a) a focus for the research questions or hypotheses that were investigated and
   (b) guidelines for an appropriate methodology and design

As you can see from this list of functions, they form a clear and logical outline for the literature review. Understanding these will help you determine the type of content that is relevant to the review and guide you in how to most effectively organize it so that it reveals the 'argument' underpinning your study.

THE CONTENT AND STRUCTURE OF A THESIS LITERATURE REVIEW

The content of the review comprises a series of theme/topic units (frequently signaled by the use of headings and sub-headings like you see in a table of contents) that review the non-research literature (e.g. background and theoretical perspectives) and research literature relevant to your research project (i.e. functions 1–3 above). But, the review is more than just a summary of this material: it includes a critique of this material (i.e. function 4 above), that is, it identifies arguments for and against issues and controversies reviewed and assesses or weighs up the value of theories, ideas, claims, research designs, methods and conclusions. In doing so, it identifies gaps or shortcomings in the reported knowledge and research (i.e. function 5 above). Not all gaps will have been addressed by you in your research project, so you will need to provide a rationale for the particular focus of your study (i.e. function 6 above). In other words, you will need to explain why the gap(s) that you addressed were important and significant enough to warrant your attention. Having done this, your final task in the review will be to announce how your research project sought to answer the research questions informed by the gap(s) (i.e. function 7 above).

Although the structure of the review will vary from thesis to thesis, it will always contain an introduction, a body and a conclusion. The key decision that you will need to make will concern the organization of the material you present in the body of your review. Some of the structural options you will want to reflect on include those presented below in Box 4b.

Box 4b   Organizational options for a literature review

1. the themes and topics of the review
2. the research questions or hypotheses being addressed
3. the variables investigated in the study
4. a chronological presentation of non-research and research literature
5. a combination of these options

How you finally decide on the structure of your review will to a large extent be determined by the themes and topics of the content of the literature you have read. As we consider the content and structure of the body of the review in the next section, we will look at one approach that students have found effective. This approach enables you to determine the theme/topic units of your review while, at the same time, enabling you to develop a structural pattern for their inclusion in the review. There is no right or wrong way of going about this process so you may want to modify the approach that is given to suit your own needs.

The body of the literature review

In this section, we will be focusing on the macro and micro-structure of the review: (1) how to determine the theme/topic units that will be included in your review and (2) how to construct a theme/topic unit. As we consider the macro structure, we will look at three stages that can be followed in determining what the theme/topic units will be: (a) keeping a record/summary of the relevant literature; (b) developing a mind-map of key themes/topics and (c) creating a table of contents. In focusing on the micro-structure of a single theme/topic unit, we will look at a range of discourse move options and analyze the extent to which they have been employed in units from our sample thesis.

Determining thematic/topic units

1. Keep a record/summary of relevant literature

Keep a record of each piece of literature that you read and decide whether or not it is (a) directly relevant, (b) possibly relevant or (c) not relevant to the focus of your study. For each piece of literature that you have categorized as either directly or possibly relevant, keep a record of its key details in a computer file. Like the example given below in Box 4c, your summary record might include seven types of detail.

Box 4c   Summary of detail from key references

Author/Date	Dornyei, 2001	Julkuren, 2001	MacIntyre, 1998	Skehan, 1989
Focus				
Research design				
Participants/ Context				
Data collection methods				
Key findings				
Limitations				
Similarities/ Differences to other literature				

It is best to keep the detail in this type of record to a bare minimum. Some students find it useful to attach a one page summary with a little more information to a hard copy of the text that is then filed in a ring binder according to the first author's surname.

2. Develop a mind-map of key themes/topics

As you read and summarize each piece of literature, develop a mind-map of the key themes and topics that feature in this material. There may be more than one theme/topic per piece. For example, an article may focus on several questions or issues. For the first text that you read, choose a heading or title that summarizes in 1–3 words each of its key themes or topics. Place the theme/topic heading on either a large sheet of paper or on a computer spreadsheet and then write the author(s) and date of the text underneath. The mind-map example below in Box 4d illustrates this. Note that this is very much a condensed version of the full literature review mind-map.

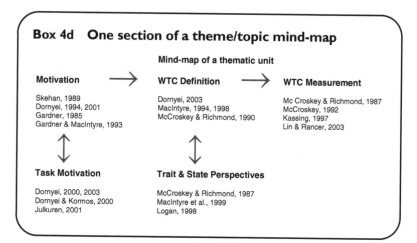

Box 4d   One section of a theme/topic mind-map

Mind-map of a thematic unit

Motivation ⟶ **WTC Definition** ⟶ **WTC Measurement**

Skehan, 1989
Dornyei, 1994, 2001
Gardner, 1985
Gardner & MacIntyre, 1993

Dornyei, 2003
MacIntyre, 1994, 1998
McCroskey & Richmond, 1990

Mc Croskey & Richmond, 1987
McCroskey, 1992
Kassing, 1997
Lin & Rancer, 2003

Task Motivation   **Trait & State Perspectives**

Dornyei, 2000, 2003
Dornyei & Kormos, 2000
Julkuren, 2001

McCroskey & Richmond, 1987
MacIntyre et al., 1999
Logan, 1998

As you read other texts on the same theme/topic, write the author(s) and date of these texts under those already included. For example, in Box 4d above, you can see that on the theme of motivation (one of the key themes in our sample thesis), several pieces of literature have been included. Whenever you read about a new theme/topic, start a new heading. If you think about the relationship between different themes/topics that you have added to the mind-map, place them in a position that reveals something about their relationship to other theme/topic headings. In the mind-map above, you can see, for example, that a new theme/topic on 'task motivation' has been added and that it has been placed under the more general theme/topic of 'motivation' with its relationship revealed through the use of a two-way arrow. The same can be seen with the 'WTC definition'. Two defining perspectives 'trait' and 'state' have been placed under it. You can also see that a one-way arrow connects the themes/topics 'motivation' and 'WTC definition' because willingness to communicate is influenced by a learner's motivation. The one-way connection between 'WTC definition' and 'measurement of WTC' suggests the logic of considering what is meant by WTC before ways in which it can be measured.

For texts that are particularly relevant to your study, you may want to also develop subsidiary themes/topics within key themes/topics. For example, in our sample thesis, one of the main themes/topics is 'empirical studies of willingness to communicate in L2'. In reading about the empirical research that has been carried out with respect to the L2 (second language), four key types of study were considered. As Box 4e below illustrates, these were presented as sub-headings on another part of the mind-map.

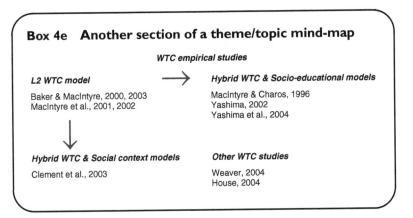

Box 4e Another section of a theme/topic mind-map

WTC empirical studies

L2 WTC model

Baker & MacIntyre, 2000, 2003
MacIntyre et al., 2001, 2002

Hybrid WTC & Socio-educational models

MacIntyre & Charos, 1996
Yashima, 2002
Yashima et al., 2004

Hybrid WTC & Social context models

Clement et al., 2003

Other WTC studies

Weaver, 2004
House, 2004

Even though the process of creating a mind-map may involve renaming and moving headings and sub-headings around, it has proven to be a time-effective approach for (a) keeping track of one's reading, (b) determining what the theme/topic units will be and (c) determining the relationship of units with one another.

3. Creating a table of contents

Once a mind-map has been created, it may be useful to produce a table of contents outline like the one shown in Box 4f below.

Box 4f Table of contents (literature review chapter)

Chapter 2 Willingness to communicate: A review of the literature

---

Box 4f   (Continued)

2.3   Task motivation
2.4   Willingness to Communicate
2.4.1   Defining Willingness to Communicate
2.4.2   Measurement of Willingness to Communicate
2.4.3   The Trait Perspective and the State Perspective of WTC
2.4.4   Cultural Contexts and their impact on WTC
2.4.5   Empirical Studies of Willingness to Communicate in L2
2.4.5.1 Test of the L2 WTC Model
2.4.5.2 Test of the Hybrid Socio-educational Model and the WTC Model
2.4.5.3 Test of the Hybrid of Social Context Model and the WTC Model
2.4.5.4 Other Empirical Studies of WTC
2.4.6   Gaps in L2 WTC Research
2.4.7   Operationalization of WTC in the Second Language Classroom
2.5   Summary

Having decided on the theme/topic units and on their relationship to one another, you will then be ready to start constructing individual theme/topic units.

Constructing a theme/topic unit

In this section, we will consider first a genre approach to the construction of a unit. In doing so, we will look at a series of move and sub-move options. This will be followed with a sample analysis of a thematic unit from our sample thesis on WTC. Here, we will focus on the moves that have been included and on some of the key linguistic characteristics of the unit. Once you have a good understanding of how one theme/topic unit has been constructed, you will be able to analyze others and think about what is the best approach for the development of each of your own theme/topic units.

1. Discourse move and sub-move options

Each theme/topic unit is made up of a series of moves and sub-moves. There are three main moves that might be included. As you will see in Box 4g, there are a number of sub-moves that might be used to develop each main move.

Box 4g   Main move and sub-move options

Moves	Sub-moves
1. Establish some aspect of the knowledge territory relevant to your research.	a. A presentation of knowledge claims and statements about theories, beliefs, constructs and definitions. b. A statement about the centrality, importance or significance of the theme/topic. c. A presentation of research evidence (e.g. findings, methodology).
2. Create a research niche/gap in knowledge.	a. A critique of knowledge claims, issues and problems associated with move 1 claims/statements. b. A presentation of research evidence in relation to move 2a. c. An identification of gap(s) in knowledge and/or research. d. A continuation or development of a tradition that has been established but not fully investigated. e. A presentation of arguments for introducing a new perspective or theoretical framework (as a result of move 1 claims/statement).
3. Announce how you will occupy the research niche/gap.	a. An announcement of the aim of the research study. b. An announcement of the theoretical position(s) or framework(s). c. An announcement of the research design and processes. d. An announcement of how you define concepts and terms in your research.

Theme/topic units are typically made up of a **series** of move 1 statements/claims. Some of these will be developed with move 2 sub-moves. For example, some move 1 claims will be critiqued and some may lead to an identification of where there are gaps or shortcomings in the area of knowledge that could be considered for investigation. Move 3 statements are less likely to feature during the presentation of a theme/topic unit. Although some authors choose to signal how they will aim to address the issue(s) raised or how they will fill a particular knowledge gap during their presentation of a unit, others will discuss them at the end of the unit or in the concluding section of the literature review.

2. Sample analysis 1 – Reporting theoretical perspectives

In this section, we will take a look at the various main moves and sub-moves used in one thematic unit of our sample thesis. The text of the unit entitled *Motivation and Willingness to Communicate* is provided in Box 4h below. If you look back at the Table of Contents presented above in Box 4f, you will see that this is the second theme/topic unit of the literature review. Before we proceed further, it would be useful for you to read this now.

Box 4h   Text of sample theme/topic unit one

2.2 Motivation and Willingness to Communicate

1. Motivation is viewed as a 'key factor in L2 learning' in second language acquisition (SLA) research (Ellis 1994: 508; Skehan 1989). 2. The study of the role of motivation in SLA has been a prominent research area in the second language field (Dörnyei and Kormos 2000). 3. The most important and influential motivation theory specific to second language learning has been proposed by Robert Gardner, Wallace Lambert and associates (Skehan 1989, Dörnyei 2001), who 'grounded motivation research in a social psychological framework' (Dörnyei 1994: 273). 4. Gardner and Lambert (1972) drew a distinction between integrative motivation and instrumental motivation. 5. Integrative motivation is identified with positive attitudes towards a target language group and a willingness to integrate into that target community. 6. Instrumental motivation, on the other hand, refers to functional and practical reasons for learning a second language, such as getting a job or a promotion, or to pass a required examination.

7. Gardner (1985) established socio-educational model to account for the role of various individual differences in the learning of a second language. 8. This model proposes two basic attitudes – integrativeness and 'attitudes toward the learning situation'. 9. Integrativeness refers to the desire to learn a second language to meet and communicate with

---

members of the L2 community whereas 'attitudes toward the learning situation' refers to learners' reaction to formal instruction (Gardner and MacIntyre 1993). 10. These two classes of variables contribute to learners' levels of L2 motivation which, in turn, influences language learning outcomes in both formal and informal learning situations (MacIntyre and Charos 1996). 11. Gardner's approach has influenced many studies in L2 motivation and has had direct empirical support in the field of second and foreign language education (Gardner 1988). 12. Yet in spite of this influence, results found in some studies were contradictory. 13. For example, studies by Oller and his associates reported negative relationships between integrativeness measures and proficiency (Skehan 1989). 14. Gardner himself had admitted that no link necessarily existed between integrative attitudes and proficiency, and also acknowledged that the patterns of relationships among attitudinal and motivational variables and learning outcomes found in various studies were unstable (1985).

15. A noticeable 'educational shift' occurred in motivation research during the 1990s, a period of feverish research activity in L2 learning motivation. 16. In particular, the period was marked by a search for new learning motivation paradigms, as well as an expansion of the scope, in both theory and practice, of L2 learning motivation. 17. The most influential pioneering works were provided by Crookes and Schmidt (1991), Dörnyei (1994), Oxford and Shearin (1994). 18. Crookes and Schmidt (1991) criticized the dominance of Gardner's social psychological approach, offering instead a motivational framework made up of four components. 19. These were interest, relevance, expectancy and satisfaction/outcome. 20. According to the authors, these variables provided an alternative to Gardner's integrative/instrumental dichotomy (Dörnyei 2001). 21. Dörnyei (1994) criticized Gardner's model because, in his view, its main emphasis relied on general motivational components grounded in a social milieu rather than in the foreign language classroom. 22. He thus called for a more pragmatic and education-centered approach to language learning motivation. 23. In this he followed an approach taken earlier by Crookes and Schmidt (1991), by examining motivation at micro, classroom, curriculum and extracurricular levels, then synthesizing them into a three-level framework – language level, learner level and learning situation level. 24. Oxford and Shearin's (1994) study addressed a growing gap between L2 motivation theories and the emerging concepts in mainstream motivational psychology.

Box 4h (Continued)

25. They argued that the integrative/instrumental view of motivation was too narrow, and offered alternative ways by which the notion of L2 motivation might be considered. 26. Yet, at the same time, they called for an expansion of the social psychological approach. 27. A common thread running through the literature mentioned above was a view suggesting that Gardner's theory was so influential and dominant, that alternative concepts were not seriously considered (Crookes and Schmidt 1991: 501; Dörnyei 1994: 274).

28. In response to criticism and calls for the adaptation of a wider vision of motivation (for example, Crookes and Schmidt 1991, Dörnyei 1994, Oxford and Shearin 1994), Tremblay and Gardner (1995) extended Gardner's earlier construct of L2 motivation and proposed a new structural model. 29. They incorporated three alternative motivational theories into the model: (i) goal theory, for which Oxford and Shearin (1994) suggested that learners' personal goals in language learning situations should be set specifically in ways that were challenging but achievable, and accompanied by appropriate feedback about progress; (ii) attribution theory, intended to explain why subjective reasons to which learners attributed their past successes and failures considerably shaped their motivational disposition (Dörnyei 2003: 8); and (iii) self-efficacy theory, in which self-efficacy refers to a learner's judgment of how well he can execute course of actions (Oxford and Shearin 1994), or an individual's beliefs that he has the ability to reach a certain level of performance (Tremblay and Gardner 1995). 30. Their model was empirically tested and supported to reveal that motivation was a socially and psychologically complex construct (Tremblay and Gardner 1995; Gardner et al. 1997).

31. The new approaches explored during the 1990s moved towards a wider direction in theorizing motivation, rather than a simple focus on the social psychological dimension (Dörnyei 1998). 32. Gardner's (1985) approach offered a macro perspective in which 'L2 motivation was examined in a broad sense, by focusing on the learners' overall and generalized disposition towards learning the L2' (Dörnyei 2002). 33. This macro perspective was however criticized as being 'less adequate for providing a fine-tuned analysis of instructed Second Language Acquisition (SLA), which takes place primarily in language classrooms' (Dörnyei 2003: 11). 34. But the 1990s movement did place greater emphasis on a more situated approach, and shifted from social attitudes to classroom reality, with more and more studies investigating how student motivation

was reflected in concrete classroom situations (Dörnyei 1994, 2002). 35. Recent research directions that have adopted this situated approach have been characterized by a micro perspective that included the study of task motivation and the study of willingness to communicate (Dörnyei 2003).

Before I provide my analysis of the text, you may like to see if you can decide what discourse main moves and sub-moves have been used in some or all of the text. You can write your move selections in the second column.

Paragraph 1

Sentences 1 and 2 (move 1b) introduce this theme/topic unit with statements about the centrality and importance of motivation in second language acquisition. Sentence 3 then introduces a key knowledge statement about the theoretical background underpinning the role of motivation in SLA (second language acquisition). The knowledge claims presented in sentences 4–6 define two key motivation constructs. Thus, three different aspects of the knowledge territory of motivation in SLA have been introduced: its importance (move 1b), its theoretical significance (move 1a) and its construct components (move 1a).

Box 4h(i)   Paragraph 1

1. Motivation is viewed as a 'key factor in L2 learning' in second language acquisition (SLA) research (Ellis 1994: 508; Skehan 1989). 2. The study of the role of motivation in SLA has been a prominent research area in the second language field (Dörnyei and Kormos 2000). 3. The most important and influential motivation theory specific to second language learning has been proposed by Robert Gardner, Wallace Lambert and associates (Skehan 1989, Dörnyei 2001), who 'grounded motivation research in a social psychological framework' (Dörnyei 1994: 273).	Move 1b (centrality, importance) Move 1b (claims)

Box 4h(i)   (Continued)

4. Gardner and Lambert (1972) drew a distinction between integrative motivation and instrumental motivation. 5. Integrative motivation is identified with positive attitudes toward a target language group and a willingness to integrate into that target community. 6. Instrumental motivation, on the other hand, refers to functional and practical reasons for learning a second language, such as getting a job or a promotion, or to pass a required examination.

Paragraph 2

In this paragraph, the author describes and explains the contribution of this early theoretical perspective before explaining that it has not gone unchallenged. She begins by presenting a number of knowledge claims (move 1a) in sentences 7–10: theoretical claims in the form of a model concerning the role of motivation in L2 learning (sentences 7, 8 and 10); and a definition of the model's two components/variables (sentence 9). These move 1a statements lead naturally to move 1c in sentence 11 where research evidence in support of the theoretical model is mentioned. Despite this evidence, sentences 12–14 introduce move 2a where the evidence presented in sentence 11 is critiqued. In sentences 12–13, the author tells us that some studies have revealed contradictory findings (note that in doing so move1c is being used to support move 2a). The author, in sentence 14, then offers a resolution to these two positions by stating that the model's designer (a) had not claimed that there is necessarily a link between one of the two variables (integrative attitudes) and L2 proficiency and (b) had acknowledged that the relationship between the two variables and learning outcomes revealed in studies were unstable. In doing so, the author is indirectly exposing a gap or an area of investigation that needs to be further investigated. She is thereby indirectly hinting at a move 2b or 2c.

Box 4h(ii) Paragraph 2

7. Gardner (1985) established socio-educational model to account for the role of various individual differences in the learning of a second language. 8. This model proposes two basic attitudes – integrativeness and 'attitudes toward the learning situation'. 9. Integrativeness refers to the desire to learn a second language to meet and communicate with members of the L2 community whereas 'attitudes toward the learning situation' refers to learners' reaction to formal instruction (Gardner and MacIntyre 1993). 10. These two classes of variables contribute to learners' levels of L2 motivation which, in turn, influences language learning outcomes in both formal and informal learning situations (MacIntyre and Charos 1996). 11. Gardner's approach has influenced many studies in L2 motivation and has had direct empirical support in the field of second and foreign language education (Gardner 1988). 12. Yet in spite of this influence, results found in some studies were contradictory. 13. For example, studies by Oller and his associates reported negative relationships between integrativeness measures and proficiency (Skehan 1989). 14. Gardner himself had admitted that no link necessarily existed between integrative attitudes and proficiency, and also acknowledged that the patterns of relationships among attitudinal and motivational variables and learning outcomes found in various studies were unstable (1985).

Move 1a (claims)

Move 1c (evidence)
Move 2a (critique)
Moves 2a/1c
(critique & evidence)

Move 2a (critique)

Paragraph 3

Paragraph 3 below then introduces us to the 'educational shift' that occurred in motivation research during the 1990s. Thus, we are presented with a chronological outline of developments in theoretical claims and with arguments about second language learning motivation. Throughout the paragraph, each of the sentences is concerned with a critique of the Gardner and associates perspectives' because of the limited nature of their focus and therefore of their sole relevance to motivation in the second language learning classroom setting. Therefore, except for sentence 24 where a 2b move refers directly to a study, the paragraph is made up of 2a and 2e moves entirely. This said, it needs to be acknowledged also that 2b moves referring generally to research activity informing the various theoretical perspectives are implied in sentences 15 and 21.

It is useful to note also the way in which the various 2a move claims are organized in the paragraph. Sentences 15–16 introduce the reader to the shift that occurred in the 1990s and the reason for its occurrence. Sentence 17 then identifies the key theorists/researchers behind the developments. Sentences 18–20 explain the focus and contribution of the first of these (Crookes & Schmidt, 1991), while sentences 21–23 introduce the work of the second (Dornyei, 1994, including a further reference to Crookes & Schmidt, 1991) and sentences 21–26 the work of the third (Oxford & Shearin, 1994). Finally, sentence 27 summarizes 'the common thread running through the literature mentioned above' – the dominance of Gardner's theory (referred to in paragraph 2), that is, to the point where other perspectives on motivation were ignored.

Box 4h(iii)   Paragraph 3

15. A noticeable 'educational shift' occurred in motivation research during the 1990s, a period of feverish research activity in L2 learning motivation. 16. In particular, the period was marked by a search for new learning motivation paradigms, as well as an expansion of the scope, in both theory and practice, of L2 learning motivation. 17. The most influential pioneering works were provided by Crookes and Schmidt	Move 2a (critique)
	Moves 2a, 2e (critique & new perspective) Move 2a (critique)
	Moves 2a, 2e (critique & new perspective)

(1991), Dörnyei (1994), Oxford and Shearin (1994). 18. Crookes and Schmidt (1991) criticized the dominance of Gardner's social psychological approach, offering instead a motivational framework made up of four components. 19. These were interest, relevance, expectancy and satisfaction/outcome. 20. According to the authors, these variables provided an alternative to Gardner's integrative/instrumental dichotomy (Dörnyei 2001). 21. Dörnyei (1994) criticized Gardner's model because, in his view, its main emphasis relied on general motivational components grounded in a social milieu rather than in the foreign language classroom. 22. He thus called for a more pragmatic and education-centered approach to language learning motivation. 23. In this he followed an approach taken earlier by Crookes and Schmidt (1991), by examining motivation at micro, classroom, curriculum and extracurricular levels, then synthesizing them into a three-level framework – language level, learner level and learning situation level. 24. Oxford and Shearin's (1994) study addressed a growing gap between L2 motivation theories and the emerging concepts in mainstream motivational psychology. 25. They argued that the integrative/instrumental view of motivation was too narrow, and offered alternative ways by which the notion of L2 motivation might be considered. 26. Yet, at the same time, they called for an expansion of the social psychological approach. 27. A common thread running through the literature mentioned above was a view suggesting that Gardner's theory was so influential and dominant, that alternative concepts were not seriously considered (Crookes and Schmidt 1991: 501; Dörnyei 1994: 274).

Moves 2a (critique)
Moves 2a, 2e
(critique & new perspective)

Moves 2a, 2b
(critique & evidence)

Moves 2a, 2e
(critique & new perspective)

Paragraph 4

Following on from the critique and call for 'a wider vision of motivation', paragraph 4 below presents the response to these move 2a claims. In sentence 28, move 2e introduces the new theoretical model proposed by Tremblay and Gardner, 1995. Sentence 29 (also move 2e) then describes the alternative motivation theories that were incorporated into the new model. Finally, in sentence 30, move 2b explains how research evidence showed that motivation was a socially and psychologically complex construct, thereby supporting the arguments expressed in paragraph 3 about the inadequacy of Gardner's original perspective.

Box 4h(iv)   Paragraph 4

28. In response to criticism and calls for the adaptation of a wider vision of motivation (for example, Crookes and Schmidt 1991, Dörnyei 1994, Oxford and Shearin 1994), Tremblay and Gardner (1995) extended Gardner's earlier construct of L2 motivation and proposed a new structural model. 29. They incorporated three alternative motivational theories into the model: (i) goal theory, for which Oxford and Shearin (1994) suggested that learners' personal goals in language learning situations should be set specifically in ways that were challenging but achievable, and accompanied by appropriate feedback about progress; (ii) attribution theory, intended to explain why subjective reasons to which learners attributed their past successes and failures considerably shaped their motivational disposition (Dörnyei 2003: 8); and (iii) self-efficacy theory, in which self-efficacy refers to a learner's judgment of how well he can execute course of actions (Oxford and Shearin 1994), or an individual's beliefs that he has the ability to reach a certain level of performance (Tremblay and Gardner 1995). 30. Their

Move 2e
(new perspective)

Move 2b (evidence)

model was empirically tested and supported to reveal that motivation was a socially and psychologically complex construct (Tremblay and Gardner 1995; Gardner et al. 1997).

Paragraph 5

In a series of 1a moves, paragraph 5 sums up the developments presented in the first four paragraphs. Starting with summary statements (sentence 31) of the overall focus of developments in the 1990s, the paragraph proceeds in sentences 32 and 33 to explain what the developments were a response to, while sentence 34 points to the significance of the developments. Sentence 35 ends the paragraph with a statement about the influence of these developments on recent research – a focus on empirically testing micro perspectives like task motivation and a willingness to communicate. Thus, the final sentence provides a link to the next thematic/topic unit of the literature review on task motivation.

Box 4h(v)   Paragraph 5

31. The new approaches explored during the 1990s moved towards a wider direction in theorizing motivation, rather than a simple focus on the social psychological dimension (Dörnyei 1998). 32. Gardner's (1985) approach offered a macro perspective in which 'L2 motivation was examined in a broad sense, by focusing on the learners' overall and generalized disposition towards learning the L2' (Dörnyei 2002). 33. This macro perspective was however criticized as being 'less adequate for providing a fine-tuned analysis of instructed Second Language Acquisition (SLA), which takes place primarily in language classrooms' (Dörnyei 2003: 11). 34. But the 1990s movement did place greater emphasis on a more situated approach, and shifted from social attitudes to classroom reality, with more and more studies investigating

Move 1a (claims)

Box 4h(v)   (Continued)

how student motivation was reflected in concrete classroom situations (Dörnyei 1994, 2002).
35. Recent research directions that have adopted
this situated approach have been characterized by
a micro perspective that included the study of
task motivation and the study of willingness to
communicate (Dörnyei 2003).

Overview of macro structure of the unit:

Now that we have examined in detail the move structure of the
unit, it is worth reflecting on its macro structure.

1. This theme/topic unit is primarily concerned with an overview
   of the development of theoretical perspectives on motivation.
2. The original perspective and model is introduced first (paragraphs 1 and 2) and is achieved by a series of move 1a claims
   and statements. However, the final sentences of paragraph 2
   draw our attention to shortcomings in this perspective for
   understanding motivation in the second language classroom.
3. A critique of this perspective and model is then developed in
   paragraph 3 by means of 2a and 2e moves.
4. The outcome of this response (an extension of the original
   model) is presented in paragraph 4 through the use of move 2e
   and research evidence offering support in a single move 2b.
5. The final paragraph then summarizes what has been presented
   in the unit with a series of 1a statements.

While the theoretical perspectives underpinning the research that
is being reported in a thesis occupy a noteworthy component of a
literature review, an even greater consideration is generally given
to a review of the research that has been carried out in the area of
investigation – research that may have focused on validating theoretical perspectives and research that has examined the effect of
certain conditions and variables on the issue or problem that was

central to the study. Our analysis so far has looked at the discourse patterning of a thematic unit primarily concerned with one aspect of the theoretical underpinning of the study conducted in our sample thesis. It is also important to analyze the way in which empirical research can be presented in a thematic/topic unit. So, we are now going to look at how this was achieved in another unit from our sample thesis entitled 'Cultural contexts and their impact on WTC'.

3. Sample analysis 2 – Reporting research (1)

In this section, we will analyze the discourse structure of another theme/topic unit from our sample thesis that considered the impact of one variable on a learner's willingness to communicate in the classroom. Compared with the theoretical focus of the unit discussed above, this unit is very much concerned with presenting the findings of empirical investigations into the effect of cultural contexts on WTC. For reasons of space, a shortened version of the unit will be considered. Where paragraphs have been omitted, the opening sentence of each of these paragraphs is provided so that you can see the overall argument of the unit. The shortened text is provided in Box 4i below. You will note that sentences have only been numbered for the paragraphs we will be focusing on, namely paragraphs 1, 2, 7, 8, 9 and 10. Again, I would suggest that you read the text first and then do your own move analysis before reading the analysis provided.

Box 4i   Text of sample theme/topic two

2.4.4 Cultural Contexts and Their Impact on WTC

1. As developed by McCroskey and Richmond (1987), the WTC scale was tested over time in a variety of situations, with several studies using culture as a basis. 2. In such studies, WTC in L1 was identified as a behavioral variable in one culture (for example, Asian cultures) in comparison with western culture (McCroskey and Richmond 1990). 3. The presumed impact of culture on WTC was expected to operate more at a trait than a situational level (Barraclough, Christophel and McCroskey 1988).

Box 4i   (Continued)

4. Barraclough et al. (1988) compared the results on the WTC scale of a group of college students from Australia (n = 195) with results obtained from the American sample (McCroskey and Baer 1985), in an attempt to identify similarities existing in the characteristics of WTC across the two cultures. 5. The variables tested included communication apprehension, perceived communication competence and willingness to communicate. 6. The results indicated, however, that norms generated in the United States could not be applied elsewhere without specific cultural adaptation. 7. Nevertheless, the associations among the variables observed in the United States were not unique to that country's culture, since greater WTC was associated with lower apprehension and higher perceived competence in both samples. 8. The results also indicated that American college students were significantly more willing to communicate than were similar students in Australia. 9. This finding also corresponded with that of another comparative study – American college students were found to be significantly more willing to communicate than students in Sweden (Daun, Burroughs and McCroskey 1988).

Burroughs and Marie (1990) conducted a study to examine the relationships between communication competence, communication apprehension, WTC and introversion of college students in Micronesia (n = 159). The focus of the study was on differences between data generated in the United States (McCroskey and Baer 1985) and Micronesian data.

McCroskey and Richmond (1990), taking the view that an understanding of the cultural impact on individual differences should be a vital component in the study of intercultural communication, undertook an analysis by drawing on data from other research projects conducted in Australia, Micronesia, Puerto Rico, the United States and Sweden (Barraclough et al. 1988; Burrough et al. 1990; McCroskey et al. 1985; McCroskey and Baer 1985; McCroskey et al. 1990.)

A further comparative study was carried out by Hackman and Barthel-Hackman (1993a) between New Zealand subjects and an American sample.

McDowell and Yotsuyanagi (1996) conducted a study to investigate possible differences in the level of communication apprehension and willingness to communicate by focusing on individualistic and collective cultures.

10. A study carried out by Asker attempted to apply the WTC scale – 'devised originally with American native speakers in mind' (1998: 164) – to an eastern culture. 11. The participants in this study were 124 undergraduate students in Hong Kong. 12. Some real difficulties were encountered in making cross-cultural comparisons because both the United States and Australian cases were different; in each of these countries English was not a second language, and comparisons with Sweden and Finland were difficult since the linguistics and cultural closeness between Swedish/Finnish and English were obviously greater than between English and Asian languages. 13. When taken at face value, it is tempting to conclude, on the basis made of comparisons of WTC scores attained by students with eastern cultural backgrounds with those of their western counterparts, that the comparatively low WTC scores attained by Asian students are a reflection of cultural influences, and that one-on-one communications posed difficulties not encountered in other cultures. 14. But caution should be exercised in making such broad generalizations (Asker 1998: 168).

15. Strohmaier (1997) conducted a study to investigate how communication apprehension, willingness to communicate and cultural difference interrelated in the university classroom. 16. The study also attempted to address the role of culture, and recognition of cultural differences in the communication interaction between instructors and students. 17. The participants were students enrolled in Basic English and communication classes (n = 663) and the instructors of these classes. 18. The findings pointed to an important role for culture in the interaction between culturally different students and their instructors. 19. The role of culture appeared to be an even more important factor when cultural differences existed between students and instructors. 20. The instructors were found to label the students as communicatively apprehensive or unwilling to communication with little insight into the phenomenon and treated the students differently on the basis of such labels. 21. Strohmaier's study differed from the aforementioned research in that it explored the impact of culture on WTC by examining the student–instructor interaction.

22. Wen and Clément (2003) made an attempt to adapt MacIntyre et al.'s (1998) WTC model to the Chinese ESL context. 23. They argued that Confucianism, which underlay Chinese cultural values, was likely to be manifested in L2 communication. 24. Thus WTC in the L2 in a Chinese classroom setting would be a far more complicated notion than that reflected in MacIntyre et al.'s model. 25. Their modification of the

---

Box 4i   (Continued)

structural relationships between the constructs mainly concerned two variables from the top three layers in the original model, namely, the desire to communicate (Layer III) and WTC (Layer II). 26. A distinction was made between these two notions. Desire to communicate refers to a deliberate choice or preference whereas WTC emphasizes the readiness to act. 27. The authors contended that having the desire to communicate did not necessarily imply a willingness to communicate. 28. They also suggested that a number of factors that located distally in MacIntyre et al.'s model would intervene between the links of these two variables. 29. These factors, including the societal context, personality factors, motivational orientations and affective perceptions, would be positively related as well as culturally bounded to help create a positive communication environment. 30. Remaining untested and awaiting for empirical research to confirm or disconfirm the influences of the proposed variables on WTC, this revised theoretical framework proposed a new way to localize the original WTC model in a different English as a Foreign Language (EFL) setting where variables affecting WTC could be examined from a cultural perspective.

31. In summary, both theoretical and empirical studies in the above section demonstrated that the relationship between WTC in LI and its various antecedents were substantially different when considered from a cross-cultural perspective. 32. Thus an individual's communication norms and competencies are 'reflected in the personality of a culture' (McCroskey and Richmond 1991: 31), and 'culture and communication are inextricably bound' (McDowell and Yotsuyanagi 1996: 6). 33. It was also suggested that theoretically cultural values in LI should exert an influence on WTC in L2 in an ESL setting (Wen and Clément 2003). 34. Whether they do so, however, appears to be a question yet to be addressed.

Paragraph I

As you can see from Box 4i(i) below, we have three move 1a statements introducing us to the empirical research that has looked at the impact of culture as a variable. In the first sentence, we learn that culture was one of the variables that was investigated when the

WTC scale, developed by McCroskey and Richmond (1987), tested its capacity to measure an individual's willingness to communicate. Sentence 2 explains that, in L1 (first language) contexts, culture was a behavioural variable. So, in sentence 3, the author adds that it was also expected to occur more at a trait level than at a situational level. The extent to which research evidence supports these statements/claims is therefore the focus of the rest of the unit.

Box 4i(i)   Paragraph I

1. As developed by McCroskey and Richmond (1987), the WTC scale was tested over time in a variety of situations, with several studies using culture as a basis. 2. In such studies, WTC in LI was identified as a behavioral variable in one culture (for example, Asian cultures) in comparison with western culture (McCroskey and Richmond 1990). 3. The presumed impact of culture on WTC was expected to operate more at a trait than a situational level (Barraclough, Christophel and McCroske 1988).

Move Ia (claim)

Paragraphs 2, 7 and 8

As the text below in Box 4i(ii) shows, each of the sentences in the paragraphs provides move 1c statements about a number of research studies but what is worthy of further examination with these paragraphs is the type of content that the author has provided. When each study is described and discussed, the following details (as shown in the text below) are frequently presented:

a. Author(s) and date
b. Focus of study – aim or purpose
c. Sample size and setting/location
d. Key findings
e. Discussion
f. Comparison with other studies

Box 4i(ii)   Paragraphs 2, 7 and 8

4. Barraclough et al. (1988) compared the results on the WTC scale of a group of college students from Australia (n = 195) with results obtained from the American sample (McCroskey and Baer 1985), in an attempt to identify similarities existing in the characteristics of WTC across the two cultures.
5. The variables tested included communication apprehension, perceived communication competence and willingness to communicate. 6. The results indicated, however, that norms generated in the United States could not be applied elsewhere without specific cultural adaptation. 7. Nevertheless, the associations among the variables observed in the United States were not unique to that country's culture, since greater WTC was associated with lower apprehension and higher perceived competence in both samples. 8. The results also indicated that American college students were significantly more willing to communicate than were similar students in Australia. 9. This finding also corresponded with that of another comparative study – American college students were found to be significantly more willing to communicate than students in Sweden (Daun, Burroughs and McCroskey 1988).

10. A study carried out by Asker attempted to apply the WTC scale – 'devised originally with American native speakers in mind' (1998: 164) – to an eastern culture. 11. The participants in this study were 124 undergraduate students in Hong Kong. 12. Some real difficulties were encountered in making cross-cultural comparisons because both the United States and Australian cases were different; in each of these countries English was not a second language, and comparisons

Move 1c throughout
Authors, date
Focus
Sample, location

Focus
Findings

Comparison

Author, date, focus
Sample, location
Discussion &
comparison

with Sweden and Finland were difficult since the linguistics and cultural closeness between Swedish/Finnish and English were obviously greater than between English and Asian languages. 13. When taken at face value, it is tempting to conclude, on the basis made of comparisons of WTC scores attained by students with eastern cultural backgrounds with those of their western counterparts, that the comparatively low WTC scores attained by Asian students are a reflection of cultural influences, and that one-on-one communications posed difficulties not encountered in other cultures. 14. But caution should be exercised in making such broad generalizations (Asker 1998: 168).

Discussion

15. Strohmaier (1997) conducted a study to investigate how communication apprehension, willingness to communicate and cultural difference interrelated in the university classroom. 16. The study also attempted to address the role of culture, and recognition of cultural differences in the communication interaction between instructors and students. 17. The participants were students enrolled in Basic English and communication classes (n = 663) and the instructors of these classes. 18. The findings pointed to an important role for culture in the interaction between culturally different students and their instructors. 19. The role of culture appeared to be an even more important factor when cultural differences existed between students and instructors. 20. The instructors were found to label the students as communicatively apprehensive or unwilling to communication with little insight into the phenomenon and treated the students differently on the basis of such labels. 21. Strohmaier's study differed from the aforementioned research in that it explored the impact of culture on WTC by examining the student–instructor interaction.

Author, date, focus

Focus

Sample

Findings

Discussion

Comparison

Paragraph 9

This paragraph Presented in Box 4i(iii) introduces us to a study that has not been completed. It explains the focus of the study and presents the various arguments that underpin it. In doing so, the author has employed a series of 2e moves that focus essentially on theoretical and construct statements. Had the empirical evidence been reported, many of these 2e moves would have been presented as 1c moves that focused on findings and discussion.

Box 4i(iii)   Paragraph 9

22. Wen and Clément (2003) made an attempt to adapt MacIntyre et al.'s (1998) WTC model to the Chinese ESL context. 23. They argued that Confucianism, which underlay Chinese cultural values, was likely to be manifested in L2 communication. 24. Thus WTC in the L2 in a Chinese classroom setting would be a far more complicated notion than that reflected in MacIntyre et al.'s model. 25. Their modification of the structural relationships between the constructs mainly concerned two variables from the top three layers in the original model, namely, the desire to communicate (Layer III) and WTC (Layer II). 26. A distinction was made between these two notions. Desire to communicate refers to a deliberate choice or preference whereas WTC emphasizes the readiness to act. 27. The authors contended that having the desire to communicate did not necessarily imply a willingness to communicate. 28. They also suggested that a number of factors that located distally in MacIntyre et al.'s model would intervene between the links of these two variables. 29. These factors, including the societal context, personality factors, motivational orientations and affective perceptions, would be positively related as well as culturally bounded to help create a positive communication environment. 30. Remaining untested and awaiting for empirical research to confirm or disconfirm the influences of the proposed variables on WTC, this revised theoretical framework proposed a new way

Move 2e throughout

to localize the original WTC model in a different English as a Foreign Language (EFL) setting where variables affecting WTC could be examined from a cultural perspective.

Paragraph 10

Sentences 31 and 32 in Box 4i(iv) provide summary statements of what has been presented in the preceding paragraphs. Sentence 33 explains what has yet to be discovered but provides an argument, using move 2e, about what could reasonably be expected in a study that examined the effect of the cultural variable on second language learners' willingness to communicate in an ESL setting. Finally, sentence 34 makes this gap/research niche explicit.

Box 4i(iv)   Paragraph 10

31. In summary, both theoretical and empirical studies in the above section demonstrated that the relationship between WTC in LI and its various antecedents were substantially different when considered from a cross-cultural perspective. 32. Thus an individual's communication norms and competencies are 'reflected in the personality of a culture' (McCroskey and Richmond 1991: 31), and 'culture and communication are inextricably bound' (McDowell and Yotsuyanagi 1996: 6). 33. It was also suggested that theoretically cultural values in LI should exert an influence on WTC in L2 in an ESL setting (Wen and Clément 2003). 34. Whether they do so, however, appears to be a question yet to be addressed.

Move 1a (claim)

Move 2e (new perspective)

Move 2c (gap)

Overview of macro structure of the unit:

1. We have seen that introductory background statements have been offered in the first paragraph of this thematic/topic unit through the use of move 1a statements and that the following

87

paragraphs are devoted to the presentation of the available research evidence by means of move 1c statements.

2. The author has also introduced us to a series of move 2e statements in which she explains another direction that has yet to be fully investigated.

3. The unit concludes with both a summary of what has been presented in the unit (by means of move 1a statements) and a statement (using move 2e) about what might be expected from another piece of research into the effect of culture as a variable in the WTC of ESL settings. In doing so, the author is indicating a research niche or gap that has yet to be investigated. One would expect, therefore, that this might at least be part of the focus of the study being reported in the thesis.

4. We have seen in this unit that each of the empirical studies has been reported in quite a lot of detail. It is also the case in a literature review that less attention might be given to such detail especially if the focus of the research has less of a bearing on the central focus of the study being reported in the thesis. To illustrate this, we will have a look at one paragraph, presented below in Box 4j, from another part of our sample thesis.

3. Sample analysis 3 – Reporting research (2)

In this paragraph, the author presents in a very concise manner some of the key research findings on the extent to which a WTC scale is able to measure 'a personality-based, trait-like predisposition'. We can see that sentences 1 and 2 introduce the scale and what it aimed to measure (move 1a). Sentence 3 then refers to the findings of three studies (move 1c) but does not provide any other detail about the studies. An explanation of what the findings mean (move 1a) is then presented in the first part of sentence 4 and this is then followed up with a reference to the findings of two studies (move 1c) that support the claim. By means of a claim from two researchers, sentence 5 introduces a further reason (move 1a) for the belief that the WTC scale is the best available instrument for measuring the trait – its reliability and validity. Supporting this belief, sentence 5 refers to studies (move 1c) in the USA that found high levels of reliability. Sentence 7 introduces the fact that there is also research support (move 1a) for the construct and content validity of the instrument. Then, sentences 8 and 9 refer to research support (moves 1c) for the validity of the measure. Thus, it can be seen that the paragraph is focusing on the findings of a range of studies without reference to other features of the research and does so in a very concise, focused manner. The reader does not need further detail about the studies in a paragraph that is focused on establishing the value of the instrument.

Box 4j   Example of reporting research

1. One measure, a willingness to communicate scale, developed by McCroskey and Richmond, attempted to assess 'a personality-based, trait-like predisposition which is relatively consistent across a variety of communication contexts and any types of receivers' (1987: 5). 2. The scale was intended to measure the extent to which a person was willing to communicate and it included items related to four communication contexts – public speaking, talking at meetings, talking in small groups and talking in dyads with three types of receivers – strangers, acquaintances and friends. 3. Results of studies using the WTC scale (McCroskey and Baer 1985; McCroskey and McCroskey 1986a, b) suggested that an individual willing to communicate in one context with one receiver type was highly correlated with willingness to communicate in other contexts and with other receiver types. 4. This did not mean, however, that an individual was equally willing to communicate in all contexts and with all types of receivers, and research directed at considering the relationship generally found that the larger the number of receivers, and the more distant the relationship between the individual and the receiver(s), the less willing an individual was to communicate (McCroskey and Richmond 1991; McCroskey 1992). 5. Yet the WTC scale appeared to offer the best instrument, for reliability and validity, in measuring the WTC

Move 1a (claim)

Move 1c (evidence)

Moves 1a, 1c
(claim & evidence)

Move 1a (claim)

Box 4j (Continued)

construct (McCroskey and Richmond 1987). 6. Studies conducted in the United States found high levels of reliability; and furthermore, reliability estimates generated from both western and eastern cultures (in L1) appeared to be consistent with those obtained in the United States (McCroskey 1992, Asker 1998). 7. In addition, a number of research studies provided some support for its construct and content validity. 8. McCroskey (1992: 21) concluded that the assumptions underlying the WTC instrument were tenable and that the content validity appeared to be satisfactory. 9. Similarly, Asker (1998: 166) claimed that the content validity of the data in his study seemed to be satisfactory and consistent with findings from other studies.

Move 1c (evidence)

Move 1a (claim)
Move 1c (evidence)

Summary – body of the literature review

From the above analyses and discussion, we are now in a position to summarize the key elements of the body of the literature review before considering the conclusion and introduction.

1. The body of the review has provided the reader with an understanding of non-research (especially theoretical) and research literature relevant to the study presented in the thesis.
2. In doing so, it has drawn our attention to what is known and what is not known about the area of knowledge.
3. At times, it has identified shortcomings in the theoretical arguments and the research that has been reported, thereby revealing directly or indirectly where further thinking and research could be considered.
4. Having achieved functions 1–4 and, to some extent, function 5 (outlined in Box 4g) across a number of thematic/topic units, the reader has been prepared for announcements by the thesis author about the gap(s)/shortcoming(s) her research project

sought to investigate and why it/they were sufficiently important and significant to address.

5. The identification and justification of the research niche and the introduction to the aims and design/methodology of the project are typically presented as part of the literature review.

CONCLUSION OF THE LITERATURE REVIEW

The conclusion of the literature review will usually start with a summary of the key claims that have been presented in the various thematic/topic units of the body of the review. In doing so, the author will usually draw some conclusions about the claims. For example, this will often involve an evaluation or weighing up of the importance and significance of the claims in light of the theoretical and research literature that has been presented. Thus, moves 1a,b,c and moves 2a,b will usually feature in this discussion. Having done this, the author will identify gaps or shortcomings in this literature and explain why one or more of the gaps should be filled. One or more of the other move 2 sub-moves c,d,e will be employed for this purpose. Finally, the conclusion will introduce the reader to some of the key elements of the project. Typically, this will involve an announcement of the aim(s) and/or research question(s) of the study; an outline of the key theoretical perspectives underpinning the study; key elements of its methodology, design and processes; and possibly a consideration of how key concepts and terms have been defined. Box 4k below summarizes these characteristics.

Box 4k Characteristics and move options summary	
Characteristics	**Move options**
Summary and **conclusion** of claims (**evaluating/weighing up** importance and significance of claims in light of theory and research literature)	Moves 1a,b,c and 2a,b

---

Box 4k   (Continued)

Characteristics	Move options
Identification of **gap(s)** in knowledge and **rationale** for research project	Moves 2c,d,e
Announcements about key elements of research project (aims/research questions; theoretical perspectives; methodology, design, processes; and definitions)	Move 3a,b,c,d

---

Our next task is to consider the extent to which the conclusion of our sample thesis observed these characteristics and moves options. Again, I would suggest that you read the text below in Box 4L and try to identify which of these characteristics and moves have been used by the author.

Box 4l   Text of sample conclusion

1. This chapter has reviewed literature concerned with three areas of critical importance in this present research. 2. Firstly, the literature that addresses motivation, with a particular focus on the development of motivational research – the shift from a macro social psychological approach to a micro situated approach to motivation – was described. 3. Two research paradigms, as being representative of this situated approach to motivation, were identified as task motivation and willingness to communicate. 4. A consideration of task motivation research then followed. 5. It also presented the WTC construct and examined it from differing perspectives. 6. Empirical studies that explored the potential antecedents and consequences of WTC in L2 were reviewed. 7. Finally it foreshadows the operationalization of the WTC construct as an appropriate variable for study in a second language classroom. 8. This contention is based on observations made in the earlier literature concerned with WTC.

9. WTC has enjoyed growing interest among language learning researchers in recent years. 10. Factors such as motivation, attitudes, perceived competence and language anxiety have been found to play a

---

role in determining WTC. 11. Empirical evidence has also shown that cultural context has an impact on the relationship between WTC and its antecedents.

12. Yet it should be pointed out that, until now, very little empirical research concerning WTC in L2 appears to have been done using a combination of quantitative and qualitative methods. 13. Because of the predominant use of questionnaires, WTC research to date has tended to focus on reported WTC rather than actual classroom behavior. 14. A number of researchers have actually called for verification of self-report WTC data by behavioral studies of the L2 classroom (MacIntyre and Charos 1996; MacIntyre et al. 2001a; MacIntyre et al. 2002; Yashima 2002; Yashima et al. 2004). 15. Moreover, variations in WTC over time that would, on the face of it, inject a dynamic aspect into WTC research, appear to have been largely ignored in previous studies. 16. Moreover, further research concerned with how WTC changes over time appears to be needed.

17. This study is an attempt to fill these gaps by exploring learners' WTC behavior in a second language classroom within a task-based framework. 18. Four key research questions are thus raised below to investigate whether an individual learner's WTC behavior changes according to three different situational contexts in a second language classroom over a period of a second language course as well as exploring factors that might affect WTC behavior from learners' perspective.

1. Does learners' self-report of WTC correspond to their behavior in class in three interactional contexts: whole class, small groups and pair work?
2. Does learners' WTC behavior in class differ according to three different contexts: whole class, small groups and pair work?
3. Does learners' WTC behavior in class change over time; in the case of this study, a one-month course?
4. What are learners' perceptions of most important factors contributing to their WTC in three classroom contexts?

Paragraph 1

Sentences 1–6 are a summary of the main themes/topics presented in the body of the review but not a summary of the key claims. Sentence 7 foreshadows the various gaps that are presented later in paragraph 3 and sentence 8 reminds the reader that the contention has been justified in the body of the review. No attempt has been made to draw any conclusions about the claims that have been presented in the review. A stronger opening to the conclusion would have been provided if the key claims had been summarized and then evaluated in terms of their theoretical and empirical importance and significance before the literature gaps were identified.

Paragraph 2

By means of 1a and 1c moves, respectively, sentence 9 points to the centrality of WTC research in recent years before identifying some key findings from the literature in sentences 10 and 11. It is questionable whether or not this paragraph would have been more effectively placed before paragraph 1. Had the summary of paragraph 1 referred to claims rather than a list of themes/topics, it would have had greater rhetorical effectiveness by following paragraph which was about the centrality of research on WTC.

Paragraph 3

This paragraph, in all sentences, summarizes the various gaps (move 2b) that have been identified in the body of the review. It points out the various shortcomings in the methodological approaches that have been employed in WTC research, suggesting that these, together with a longitudinal focus (sentence 16), should be investigated.

Paragraph 4

Sentence 17 then explains that the research project being reported in the thesis investigated the gaps identified in paragraph 3 and that the methodological framework informing the project was task-based. Finally, sentence 18 announces the aims and the 4 research questions that guided the study, together with the context and duration of the investigation. Thus, moves 3 a, b and c have been included, to some extent, in this paragraph. Other theses will sometimes provide more detail about each of the four sub-moves of move 3. The extent to which this is done is usually determined by the extent to which the introduction of the methodology chapter makes these announcements. Your supervisor will be able to guide you on what might be the best approach for your thesis.

Evaluating the effectiveness of the conclusion provided in our sample thesis, it would be fair to say that apart from the lack of conclusions drawn about the claims made in the literature and the somewhat scant attention given to move 3 announcements at the end, the conclusion satisfies many of the characteristics and move options presented in Box 4k above.

Before concluding this chapter, we need to turn our attention to the Introduction of the literature review chapter.

Introduction to the literature review

Although the introduction to the literature review is placed before the body of the review, it is often the last part of the chapter to be written. An initial outline is sometimes written while the body of the review is being prepared and may then be modified once the rest of the chapter has been written. The primary function of the introduction is to give the reader an overview of the main themes/topics that will be presented in the body of the review. It is often referred to as an 'advance organizer'. Some authors, when introducing the key theme/topic units, will go beyond a listing of the units and explain the relationship between each of them and so introduce the reader to the central 'argument' of the review. As you read the introduction to our sample thesis below in Box 4m, you can think about whether it might have been a more effective introduction if the author had made more explicit connections between the various units/sections.

Box 4m   Text of sample introduction

This chapter reviews the literature associated with the main areas of interest in this study. These areas are firstly, motivation and willingness to communicate; second, task motivation; third, the willingness to

---

Box 4m   (Continued)

communicate construct (WTC); and finally, research studies concerned with willingness to communicate in L1 and L2.

The first section identifies the literature that explains the relationship between motivational research and the study of willingness to communicate. For decades, Gardner's (1972, 1980, 1985) social psychological approach to motivation was dominant until a situated educational approach (offered, for example, by Crookes and Schmidt 1991; Dörnyei 1994; Oxford and Shearin 1994) was called for in the period of motivation renaissance during the 1990s (Dörnyei 2001). The study of willingness to communicate represents an aspect of a trend moving in this direction.

The second section presents a newly developed research paradigm, and the major contributors to its development (for example, Julkunen 1989, 2001; Dörnyei 2003); that is, the so-called situated approach to motivation, referred to as task motivation.

In the third section, the WTC construct is defined at the outset from the literature, followed by a description of well-established measurements of WTC (for example, McCroskey and Richmond 1987).

The WTC construct is then considered from differing perspectives including trait, state and cultural perspectives. Empirical studies of WTC in L2, as well as the operationalisation of WTC in L2, are also considered in this section.

SOME KEY LINGUISTIC FEATURES OF THESIS LITERATURE REVIEWS AND APPROACHES TO PROCESSING THE LITERATURE

As you have seen, the literature review provides the reader with the background to fully understand (a) the context of your study and (b) why it was worth doing. In doing this, the 'argument' or 'case' that is developed throughout the literature review reports on and critiques a range of published literature (e.g. theoretical perspectives and empirical research). The skills that are required to do this effectively are several so this section will outline some of the major ones. Although they are being presented in this chapter alone, they are not only relevant to the writing of a good literature review. They will also need to be considered when you write other chapters.

Summarizing (paraphrasing and coherence)

You will be reporting on a wide range of literature in your review but only some of this will need to be discussed in detail. That which is most central to the focus of your study is likely to receive a detailed close-up consideration while other material may be synthesized more concisely. Most of your summary writing will involve paraphrasing (expressing ideas in your own words) what the literature has reported. Sometimes you may find it useful to directly quote what the literature has said. The skills for doing this will be referred to below. When directly quoting another source, it is very important to make sure that you integrate the quotation into the structure of your own writing and that you do so with grammatical accuracy. It is also important that your writing and paraphrasing provide the reader with coherent text. Avoiding convoluted sentences that may lose grammatical accuracy and therefore comprehensible meaning is one way of achieving coherence. If the reader gets to the end of a long sentence and cannot see how its ending ultimately relates to the way in which it began, you are likely to have created a convoluted sentence. Explicit rather than vague writing will also contribute to coherent text. If you take another look at any of the passages of text from our sample thesis, you will see that the author has paraphrased effectively, created coherent text and presented us with clear summary statements of the published literature.

Synthesizing (cohesion)

Synthesizing what you have read so that you can show similarities and differences in the ideas that are being discussed also requires that you draw upon the skills referred to above. Additionally, cohesive links between ideas (within and across paragraphs) need to be clear to the reader so he or she can follow your argument or narrative as you present one piece of information after another. Most often the connection between one proposition and another will be evident by content links but there are a number of linguistic devices that you can also use to strengthen the cohesion of your writing. In Box 4n below, some of these possibilities are presented, with examples from the text we referred to before and which is provided again in Box 4o.

Box 4n Some cohesive techniques with examples from Box 4m

Techniques	Examples & sentence numbers
Repetition of key word	Scale (sentences 1 & 2) *One measure, a willingness to communicate* **scale**, *developed by . . . (1)* *The* **scale** *was intended to measure (2)*
Repetition of key word	Reliability (sentences 5 & 6) *Yet the WTC scale appeared to offer the best instrument, for* **reliability** *and validity . . . (5)* *Studies . . . found high levels of* **reliability** *. . . (6)*
Addition connector	Furthermore (sentence 6) *Studies . . . found high levels of reliability; and* **furthermore**, *reliability estimates generated . . . appeared . . .* This (sentence 4 referring to sentence 3)
Pronoun reference	*Results . . . suggested that . . . (3)* **This** *did not mean . . . (4)*

Other cohesive techniques might include (1) contrast connectors (e.g. however, nevertheless, besides), (2) result connectors (e.g. therefore, consequently, thus) and (3) synonyms (words of similar meaning).

Box 4o   Text illustrating cohesive techniques

1. One measure, a willingness to communicate scale, developed by McCroskey and Richmond, attempted to assess 'a personality-based, trait-like predisposition which is relatively consistent across a variety of communication contexts and any types of receivers' (1987: 5). 2. The scale was intended to measure the extent to which a person was willing to communicate and it included items related to four communication contexts – public speaking, talking at meetings, talking in small groups and talking in dyads with three types of receivers – strangers, acquaintances and friends. 3. Results of studies using the WTC scale (McCroskey and Baer 1985; McCroskey and McCroskey 1986a, b) suggested that an individual willing to communicate in one context with one receiver type was highly correlated with willingness to communicate in other contexts and with other receiver types. 4. This did not mean, however, that an individual was equally willing to communicate in all contexts and with all types of receivers, and research directed at considering the relationship generally found that the larger the number of receivers, and the more distant the relationship between the individual and the receiver(s), the less willing an individual was to communicate (McCroskey and Richmond 1991; McCroskey 1992). 5. Yet the WTC scale appeared to offer the best instrument, for reliability and validity, in measuring the WTC construct (McCroskey and Richmond 1987). 6. Studies conducted in the United States found high levels of reliability; and furthermore, reliability estimates generated from both western and eastern cultures (in L1) appeared to be consistent with those obtained in the United States (McCroskey 1992, Asker 1998). 7. In addition, a number of research studies provided some support for its construct and content validity. 8. McCroskey (1992: 21) concluded that the assumptions underlying the WTC instrument were tenable and that the content validity appeared to be satisfactory. 9. Similarly, Asker (1998: 166) claimed that the content validity of the data in his study seemed to be satisfactory and consistent with findings from other studies.

Reporting the published literature

There are two main reasons for reporting what others have said: (1) to explain what has been reported in the literature (including what research has found) and what has not been reported (including gaps in the published literature) and (2) to evaluate or critique the work of others in order to negotiate your position/stance with respect to the existing body of knowledge. Another reason for reporting the published literature – to support your own findings – will be considered in our discussion of results chapter. Here, we will focus our attention on some of the knowledge and skills that are required for explaining what has been reported in the literature and later in this section, we will focus on the evaluation or critiquing the work of others.

(a) different approaches to reporting the published literature

Three of the main types of reporting are presented below in Box 4p with the first two examples being taken from Box 4m above and the third from Box 4q below.

Box 4p   Types of reporting with examples

Types of reporting	Examples & sentence number
Central reporting – author responsible for claim is subject of sentence	*McCroskey (1992:21) concluded that the assumptions were tenable . . . (8)*
Non-central reporting – name of author responsible for claim is placed in brackets at end of sentence	*Yet the WTC scale appeared to offer the best instrument . . . in measuring the WTC construct (**McCroskey and Richmond 1987**) (5)*
Non-reporting – less focus on author with no reporting verb such as 'argued' or 'found'	*Integrativeness refers to the desire to learn a second language . . . (**Gardner and MacIntyre 1993**) (9)*

(b) choice of reporting verb

Authors need to take care when choosing their reporting verbs. Because of the similarity in meaning between some verbs, you can easily misrepresent another author if the reporting verb is not accurate or fails to convey the exact shade of meaning intended. For example, because there is only a shade of difference in meaning between the verbs 'state' and 'claim', it is important that the appropriate and precise verb be chosen to convey what the source intended and also what you as author intend. Reflecting on the difference between verbs such as 'noted', 'stated', 'argued', 'contended', 'claimed' and 'established', it can be seen that each of these verbs conveys a greater strength of claim from 'noted' through to 'established'. In the following text in Box 4q from our sample thesis, you can see from the bold examples the range and varying strength of verbs that have been chosen to report the various claims.

Box 4q Choice of reporting verb with examples

7. Gardner (1985) **established** socio-educational model to account for the role of various individual differences in the learning of a second language. 8. This model **proposes** two basic attitudes – integrativeness and 'attitudes toward the learning situation'. 9. Integrativeness refers to the desire to learn a second language to meet and communicate with members of the L2 community whereas 'attitudes toward the learning situation' refers to learners' reaction to formal instruction (Gardner and MacIntyre 1993). 10. These two classes of variables **contribute** to learners' levels of L2 motivation which, in turn, influences language learning outcomes in both formal and informal learning situations (MacIntyre and Charos 1996). 11. Gardner's approach has **influenced** many studies in L2 motivation and has had direct empirical support in the field of second and foreign language education (Gardner 1988). 12. Yet in spite of this influence, results **found** in some studies were contradictory. 13. For example, studies by Oller and his associates **reported** negative relationships between integrativeness measures and proficiency (Skehan 1989). 14. Gardner himself had **admitted** that no link necessarily existed between integrative attitudes and proficiency, and also **acknowledged** that the patterns of relationships among attitudinal and motivational variables and learning outcomes found in various studies were unstable (1985).

(c) tense of reporting verbs

Even within a single paragraph, the choice of tenses for reporting claims or propositions can vary a great deal. Reasons for using particular tenses are presented in Box 4r below.

Box 4r   Reasons for choice of tense

Tense	Simple example	Reasons
Present simple	Smith (2008) **reveals** that . . .	To convey the current state of knowledge, make a generalization and present earlier findings as accepted facts
Past simple	Smith (2008) **revealed** that . . .	To refer to a claim or finding that has been made
Present perfect	Smith (2008) **has revealed** that . . .	To refer to the currently accepted state of affairs

---

In Box 4s below, the tenses in bold are identified. You may like to cover column two and make your own identification of tense first. Once you have checked your identification against that provided in column two, think about which reason may have informed the author's choice in each case.

Box 4s   Examples of tense choice in sample text

7. Gardner (1985) **established** socio-educational model to account for the role of various individual differences in the learning of a second language. — Past simple

8. This model **proposes** two basic attitudes – integrativeness and 'attitudes toward the learning situation'. — Present simple

9. Integrativeness **refers** to the desire to learn a second language to meet and communicate with members of the L2 community whereas 'attitudes toward the learning situation' refers to learners' reaction to formal instruction (Gardner and MacIntyre 1993). — Present simple

10. These two classes of variables **contribute** to learners' levels of L2 motivation which, in turn, influences language learning outcomes in both formal and informal learning situations (MacIntyre and Charos — Present simple

---

1996). 11. Gardner's approach **has influenced** many studies in L2 motivation and has had direct empirical support in the field of second and foreign language education (Gardner 1988). 12. Yet	Present perfect
in spite of this influence, results **found** in some studies were contradictory. 13. For example, studies by Oller and his associates **reported** negative	Past simple Past simple
relationships between integrativeness measures and proficiency (Skehan 1989). 14. Gardner himself **had admitted** that no link necessarily existed	Past perfect
between integrative attitudes and proficiency, and also **acknowledged** that the patterns of relationships among attitudinal and motivational variables	Past simple
and learning outcomes **found** in various studies were unstable (1985).	Past simple

Evaluating and critiquing the published research

As you were reading the published research for your literature review, you will have been reading it with a critical eye, thinking about the extent to which the claims that are made are justified by the evidence and so on. As you write your literature review, you need to convey these shortcomings to the reader and evaluate the extent to which the claims are valid and reasonable. You will also have thought about the appropriateness and robustness of the methodology that various studies had employed and about the way in which the methods were executed. Some of the specific questions you might like to think about as you present your review of the literature and evaluate its contribution are presented in Box 4t below.

Box 4t   Research literature evaluation questions

1. Is the research issue clearly stated?
2. Is its context sufficiently explained?
3. Is there sufficient justification for the research?
4. Are the research questions/hypotheses clearly framed?

Box 4t   (Continued)

5. Is the methodological approach relevant and comprehensive enough for these questions/hypotheses?
6. Are the methods of data collection appropriate and sufficiently wide-ranging to produce satisfactory answers?
7. Are the research instruments appropriate for the research?
8. Are the variables and constructs of the research clearly defined and scoped?
9. Are the data collection procedures sufficiently complete?
10. Are the data analysis procedures appropriate?
11. Have the data been appropriately analyzed?
12. Are the findings of the data related clearly to the research questions/hypotheses?
13. Are the findings relevant to the research questions/hypotheses?
14. Are the findings sufficient to provide satisfactory answers to the questions/hypotheses?
15. Are the claims and conclusions soundly based on the findings of the research?
16. Are the implications and applications drawn from the findings?

Taking a stance towards the published literature

Having reviewed and evaluated the published literature, you will want to make your stance towards it known to the reader. There are a number of linguistic strategies that can be employed to help you reveal your stance and these are presented in Box 4u below.

Box 4u   Linguistic strategies for evaluating published literature

Strategies	Purpose	Examples
Hedges	To withhold your full commitment to a statement	*May; might; possibly; likely; seemed to; appeared to*
Boosters	To reveal your certainty about a statement	*Clearly; definitely; without doubt*

Attitude markers	To reveal your attitude towards a statement	*Interestingly; surprisingly; unfortunately*
Engagement markers	To build a relationship with the reader	*As you can see; you will have noted that; consider whether*
Self-mentions	To make reference to the research(s)	*I; we; my; our*

Through the precise choice of verbs, you can also reveal your stance towards the published literature. Consider, for example, the difference in attitude and stance that is conveyed by the use of the verbs we considered beforehand: *noted, stated, argued, contended, claimed, established.*

You can also show the commitment of writers and researchers to their claims in the same way. Consider, for example, the differences revealed through the use of the following verbs: *suggested, asserted, admitted, maintained.*

Well-chosen adjectives can also convey your stance towards the work of others. Consider, for example, the use of the following: *a **truly innovative** design; his **enlightening** observations; this **landmark** study; this **seminal** work; this **uninspiring** result.*

FREQUENTLY ASKED QUESTIONS

1. How long should the literature review be?

This will most likely depend on whether you are writing a Masters or a Doctoral thesis. The literature review of a Doctoral thesis way well have 2–3 chapters while that of a Masters thesis may have only one chapter. Another guideline that supervisors often give their students is that the review may occupy about one third of the thesis, excluding references, appendices and so on. It is likely to be the longest chapter that you write. At the end of the day, it is important that you cover sufficient background to situate well the various issues you were investigating. If you were examining a number of variables, for example, the length of the review may be relatively lengthy in case you seek to background each variable in reasonable detail. Ultimately, this question should be asked of your supervisor.

2. How do I decide what to include and what not to include in the literature review?

The advice I give my students is that the research questions/ hypotheses must guide you in determining what is/is not relevant. You can ask yourself the following questions:

(1) Which aspect of my thesis does this literature relate to?
(2) Does it add anything new to what has been included already?

Following the mind-map approach introduced earlier in this chapter should help you decide whether or not a certain piece of literature is relevant.

3. Should I refer to methodology literature in my literature review?

The literature informing your own methodology is usually presented in the methodology chapter. However, when you are reviewing and evaluating your literature review material, you may refer to various aspects of methodology in order to explain why a claim or a finding, for example, is or is not valid and convincing. Sometimes, and this is more likely to be the case for a Doctoral thesis, a separate literature review chapter focuses on methodological issues alone.

4. If many writers/researchers have made the same claim, how many should I refer to?

Generally speaking, you would be best to refer to three or four, making sure that you include the most recent and the most significant. Concerning the latter, you would certainly want to include an earlier seminal work.

FURTHER ACTIVITIES

The following activities could be done individually, in pairs (with another thesis student or with your supervisor) or in small groups:

1. If you have read other theses as part of your literature search or can access theses in your discipline area from the library,

select the literature review from one thesis and carry out the following tasks:

(a) Paraphrase one or two paragraphs of the unit.
(b) Identify examples of the author's stance, drawing upon the strategies presented in Box 4t above.
(c) Identify the reporting verbs that the author has used and think about the extent to which you think they are appropriate.
(d) Under the headings central, non-central and non-reporting, identify examples of the way in which the literature referred to has been presented.

2. Select one of the most important journal articles you have read and do a critical evaluation of it, focusing on the questions provided in Box 4s above.
3. If you have written a draft of your literature review chapter, you could refer to the move and sub-move options presented earlier in this chapter to evaluate what you have written.
4. Do a move analysis of the following thematic unit from our sample Doctoral thesis and decide whether or not there are any noteworthy differences between this unit and others we have discussed in this chapter. Alternatively, you may want to select a unit from one of the theses you have read.

Output is the language produced by the learner. There is debate, too, over the role of output. While Krashen (1982, 1985, *inter alia*) does not see any theoretical role for output in SLA, others disagree. Gass (1997) argues that in one sense output is not actually a stage in acquisition but rather 'an overt manifestation of that process' (p. 7). The role of output in SLA has been put forward most clearly in Swain's (1985, 1995, 2000; Swain & Lapkin, 1995) Output Hypothesis which claims that producing language serves SLA in several ways.

One way output can help L2 acquisition is by developing fluency (de Bot, 1996; Skehan, 1998; Swain, 1995) or the process of proceduralization in language production (Lyster, 1998a). As learners produce the L2, they

(Continued)

become more proficient in the use of those linguistic forms. While output is seen to develop fluency, Swain (1995) also proposes that output helps learners develop linguistic accuracy through consciousness-raising and hypothesis-testing. In regards to consciousness-raising, Swain argues that output can result in the noticing of linguistic items. Such noticing is argued to be necessary for L2 acquisition (See Section 2.5 for a further discussion of noticing). Furthermore, Swain suggests that this noticing of linguistic forms can either provide new linguistic knowledge for learner or serve to consolidate already existing L2 knowledge.

The second possible function of output is hypothesis testing (Gass, 1997; Skehan, 1998; Swain, 1995). As learners become aware of new linguistic forms, they may try them out in their own production. This process can provide learners with feedback as to whether their hypotheses about the language were indeed correct or not. Swain (1995) argues that even if there is no (useful) immediate feedback, learners may still benefit from their hypothesis testing. However, if feedback does occur after output, then this may make an even greater impact on the value of hypothesis testing. Additionally, the output itself and the potential feedback following it can serve as input which feeds back into the cognitive system and targets the specific areas being hypothesised by the learner (de Bot, 1996; Gass, 1997).

Output can also force learners to process language syntactically rather than semantically (Gass, 1997; Skehan, 1998; Swain, 1995). When learners attend only to the meaning of the L2, it is argued that they do not process as deeply. Furthermore, learners do not need to understand every word and morpheme in order to get the gist of an utterance, and they also sometimes indicate understanding when in fact they have not comprehended an utterance (Hawkins, 1985; Swain, 1995). However, in producing the L2, learners are forced to process language more deeply. Swain claims that output forces learners to deeper, grammatical processing which potentially has a 'significant role in the development of syntax and morphology' (p. 128). de Bot (1996) adds that actually producing the linguistic form and making the cognitive connections for oneself is better than merely perceiving it.

FURTHER READING

If you are interested in reading some of the literature that has informed the material in this chapter, you may find the following references useful:

Cone, J., & Foster, S. (1993). *Dissertations and Theses: From Start to Finish*. Washington, DC: American Psychological Association.

Cooley, L., & Lewkowicz, J. (2003). *Dissertation Writing in Practice: Turning Ideas into Text*. Hong Kong: Hong Kong University Press.

Evans, D., & Gruba, P. (2002). *How to Write a Better Thesis*. Carlton South, Victoria: Melbourne University Press.

Galvan, J. (2009). *Writing Literature Reviews: A Guide for Students of the Social and Behavioural Sciences*. Glendale, CA: Pyrczak Publishing.

Hart, C. (1998). *Doing a Literature Review*. London: Sage.

Hart, C. (2005). *Doing Your Masters Dissertation*. London: Sage.

Hyland, K. (2000). *Disciplinary Discourses: Social Interactions in Academic Writing*. London: Longman.

Hyland, K. (2004). Disciplinary interactions: Metadiscourse in L2 postgraduate writing. *Journal of Second Language Writing, 13*, 133–151.

Hyland, K. (2005). Stance and engagement: A model of interaction in academic discourse. *Discourse Studies, 7*, 173–192.

Hyland, K., & Tse, P. (2004). Metadiscourse in academic writing: A reappraisal. *Applied Linguistics, 25*, 156–177.

Kwan, B. (2006). The schematic structure of literature reviews in doctoral theses of Applied Linguistics. *English for Specific Purposes, 25*, 30–55.

Paltridge, B., & Starfield, S. (2007). *Thesis and Dissertation Writing in a Second Language: A Handbook for Supervisors*. New York: Routledge.

Rudestam, K., & Newton, R. (2001). *Surviving Your Dissertation: A Comprehensive Guide to Content and Process*. Newbury Park, CA: Sage.

Seliger, H., & Shohamy, E. (1989). *Second Language Research Methods*. Cambridge: Cambridge University Press.

Swales, J. (2004). *Research Genres: Explorations and Applications*. Cambridge: Cambridge University Press.

5 Methodology

INTRODUCTION

In this chapter, we will be thinking about the functions of the methodology chapter, the content that should be included and how to most effectively organize it. This is often a relatively straightforward chapter to write because the issues and processes that need to be presented will have been considered before the data were collected and notes may well have been made before and during the data collection process. If care and attention have been given to this detail, the writing process should not present any difficulties. However, if you are reading this chapter while thinking about the nature and design of your study, it will be important for you to have a clear understanding of the aims and functions of the chapter. So, we will begin with an outline of its key functions before moving on to a consideration of the moves and sub-moves, some important language features, answers to some frequently asked questions and references for further reading.

THE FUNCTIONS OF A THESIS METHODOLOGY CHAPTER

You will have concluded your literature review chapter(s) with an announcement of the aims and/or research questions/hypotheses that you investigated in your study so the key aims of this chapter will be to describe and justify the methodological approach, the research design, the data collection and analytical processes you followed. The specific functions of the chapter will therefore include those presented in Box 5a below.

Box 5a Functions of a thesis methodology chapter

1. A description and justification of the **methodological approach** best suited to your research questions/hypotheses
2. A description and justification of the **research design** best suited to examine your research questions/hypotheses
3. A description and justification of the **specific methods** employed for data collection
4. A discussion of ways in which the **validity and reliability** of your data were achieved
5. A description and justification of the **data collection** procedures
6. A description and justification of the **data analysis** procedures

---

As we observed in the previous chapter where we considered the functions of a literature review, there is often a built-in logic to the order in which the functions might be achieved. This does not mean, however, that there is only one way in which the logic of the argument you present can be achieved. In the case of the methodology chapter, we will see below in our discussion of the moves and sub-moves that a logical argument can be achieved by describing and justifying the data collection processes before or after describing and justifying the design and methods employed in the study. Unlike the literature review chapter, with its series of main moves and sub-moves within theme/topic units, the methodology chapter should be seen as one overall theme/topic unit in which the moves are typically presented only once. However, in saying this, there may be occasions in which some sub-moves are presented more than once (a case in point being theses that include more than one method of data collection).

THE CONTENT AND STRUCTURE OF A THESIS METHODOLOGY CHAPTER

As you will see in Box 5b below, there are three main moves and a number of sub-move options for each of these in the methodology chapter.

Box 5b   Move and sub-move options

Moves	Sub-moves

1. Present the procedures for measuring the variables of your research	a. An overview of the methodological approach underpinning the research project
	b. An explanation of the methods of measuring the variables
	   i. defining
	   ii. describing
	c. A justification of the approach and methods
	   i. explaining acceptability
	   ii. citing previous research

2. Describe the data collection procedures	a. Describe the sample
	   i. describe the location of the sample
	   ii. describe the size of the sample
	   iii. describe the characteristics of the sample
	   iv. describe the context of the sample
	   v. describe the ethical issues
	b. Describe the instruments used for data collection
	   i. describe the tools/materials used
	   ii. describe the validity and reliability measures
	c. Describe the steps in the data collection process
	d. Justify the data collection procedures
	   i. highlight advantages and disadvantages
	   ii. justify choice in relation to research aims, questions and hypotheses

3. Elucidate the data analysis procedures	a. Outline the data analysis procedures b. Justify the data analysis procedures c. Preview results

The main moves and sub-moves presented here represent those typically found in empirically based theses. In some theses, authors may choose to present their move 2 and sub-move options before their move 1 options, so this is an issue you should think about and discuss with your supervisor. Either way, a logical argument will be possible. It is really a matter of whether or not you think an outline of the methodological approach that was taken to investigate the aims and/or research questions/hypotheses, presented at the end of your literature review, would be more effectively placed at the beginning of the chapter rather than introducing this after the data collection procedures of move 1. The second thing to note is that the lists of sub-moves presented here are quite comprehensive. However, they should not necessarily be seen as exhaustive. You may consider other sub-moves should be added in order to ensure a full description and justification of your methodology. As we have done in the previous chapters, we will now consider the ways in which the methodology chapter of our sample thesis was presented.

SAMPLE ANALYSIS OF WTC THESIS METHODOLOGY CHAPTER

In this section, we will consider the main moves and sub-moves used in the thesis, taking one section at a time.

Introduction

In reading the introduction to this chapter in Box 5c below, you can see that the paragraph presents a chronological advance organizer of the main sections of the chapter. In doing so, the author presents this information in the form of an argument.

Box 5c   Introduction of methodology chapter

1. This chapter introduces, and contains a discussion of, the methodological approach and research design best suited to examine the research

---

Box 5c   (Continued)

questions set out in Chapter 2.2. A multi-method design is proposed in order to arrive at answers to the research questions. 3. An overview of the research design then follows, beginning with an outline of the key methods employed; namely, classroom observation, structured personal interviews and self-report questionnaire surveys. 4. Given the importance of design and validity in the choice of research instruments, justification of each method used is provided. 5. The subsequent section includes an illustration of the specific process of data collection, followed by an overview of methods used for data analysis. 6. In addition, ethical issues concerning the research process are clarified. 7. The chapter concludes with a brief summary of the preceding sections.

In sentence 1, we are given more than just a concise description of the first section: we are told that this section will also explain why the methodological approach and research design have been chosen, namely, that they are the best suited to her investigation of the research questions set out at the end of the literature review chapter. This sentence leads into sentence 2 where it is revealed that a multi-method design was chosen as the most appropriate for this purpose. Sentence 3 advances the argument by explaining that the three key components of this method will then be described and sentence 4 explains that each component will be justified. Having outlined the sources of the data for answering the research questions, the author explains in sentence 5 that this will be followed up with an illustration of the specific process of data collection and an overview of how it will be analyzed. We are then told in sentence 6 that the ethical issues surrounding the study will be discussed before sentence 7 brings the chapter to a close with a summary of what the chapter has presented. Thus, there is a clear and logical structure to this paragraph and to the layout of the various sections of the thesis. Our task now is to examine these sections and see what content has been presented and to assess the extent to which its rhetorical structure is effective.

Methodological approach

We will divide this section into the following two parts: (1) the opening paragraph and the first sub-section entitled 'Integrating quantitative and qualitative approaches' and (2) the second sub-section entitled 'triangulation'. Before we consider the approach that has been taken in the first section, your first task is to read the text presented in Box 5d below and, by covering up the move analysis, see if you can identify the moves and sub-moves that have been used.

Box 5d   Text of methodological approach section I

1. Patton (1990: 39) has advocated the importance of recognizing that 'different methods are appropriate for different situations' so that designing a study appropriate for a specific situation is largely determined by the purpose of the study, the questions being investigated, and the sources available. 2. Due to the complexity of classroom reality and the limitations associated with every research method, a multiple research approach to data collection was adopted to strengthen the study design.

Moves Ici, ii
(justification)

Moves Ia, Ici
Approach &
justification)

3.2.1 Integrating Quantitative and Qualitative Approaches

3. The key issue associated with addressing a multi-method strategy is the integration of quantitative and qualitative research. 4. A quantitative approach is generally concerned with attitudes and with describing what people do (Hammersley 1992: 45). 5. Conversely, the central goal of qualitative approach is to 'document the world from the point of view of the people studied' (ibid. 45), to know 'how people define their situations' (Marshall and Rossman 1995: 40). 6. As Anderson and Poole

Move Ia (approach)

Moves Ici, ii
(justification)

Box 5d   (Continued)

(1994: 29) have pointed out, 'it is sometimes desirable to combine qualitative with quantitative research to maximize the theoretical implications of research findings'. 7. As mentioned in the previous chapter, research studies of WTC were predominantly quantitative in nature, and were useful in identifying variables that seemed to affect WTC in general. 8. Arguably,	Moves 1a, 1ci (approach & justification)
however, these objectively measured variables may be further clarified in ways that interpretative qualitative research can best offer (ibid. 29). 9. An adoption of a qualitative paradigm can allow the researcher to not only describe happenings and behaviors, but also to explore why such phenomena occur (Marshall and Rossman, 1995: 39). 10. Combining a qualitative approach with a quantitative approach in the present study would seem to offer the addition of completeness and meaning to the resultant data (ibid.).	Moves 1a, 1ci (approach & justification) Moves 1ci, ii (justification) Moves 1a, 1ci (approach & justification)
11. Although combining both approaches can reduce the potential danger from an exclusive reliance on a single research approach (Bryman 1992: 69), integration can be problematic (Brannen 1992) and practical problems can arise (Anderson and Poole 1994).	Moves 1ci, ii (justification)
12. The researcher should be extremely cautious about combining approaches, and in one view at least, it should be carried out only if it leads to a greater understanding of underlying issues (ibid. 29) and when data sets are based on the same purposes (Brannen 1992: 13). 13. It has been emphasized that the multimethod approach demands the researcher to specify precisely 'the particular aims of each method and the nature of the data that is expected to result' at the very least. 14. Care and precision are needed at all stages in the research process from designing to writing up (ibid. 16). 15. As Bryman (1992: 63) has claimed, the integration of quantitative and qualitative research is most frequently encountered in terms of 'triangulation', a notion that will be discussed in detail in the next section.	Moves 1ci, ii (justification) Move 1b (definition)

Paragraph I

The paragraph begins this section by explaining that the methodological approach taken in a research project needs to be determined by the specific situation and the specific purposes of the study, the research questions guiding the study and the data sources available. While implying that this was the case with this study, the author is introducing us to the fact that she chose her approach with these factors in mind. In doing so, her justification for this is based on the recommendation of one expert in the field (move 1ci and 1cii). In the second sentence, she names the approach (a multi-method approach) that she took in her study and explains why it was chosen – to strengthen and overcome shortcomings associated with the complexity of collecting data in a classroom and limitations with individual methods (moves 1a and 1ci).

Paragraph 2

This paragraph details the multi-method approach taken in the study, beginning in sentence 3 with the issue of integrating quantitative and qualitative approaches. Thus, we begin with a 1a move that also includes sentences 4 and 5. This is followed up with justification 1ci and 1cii moves in sentence 6 for combining the two approaches. A further justification is introduced in sentence 7 with reference to previous approaches that have been taken in WTC research. While it is explained that only one of these approaches (quantitative) was adopted in earlier WTC research, it is also suggested that the single approach was nevertheless appropriate. However, in sentence 8, the author explains that the inclusion of the second approach (qualitative) would be expected to throw further light on the quantitative findings. Thus, both sentences 7 and 8 employ move 1ci and hint at move 1a. The justification provided in sentence 8 is further explained in sentence 9 by means of 1ci and 1cii moves. The paragraph concludes with an explicit application of these claims to the author's study (move 1a) and a statement of justification (move 1ci).

Paragraph 3

Having advocated the advantages of combining qualitative and quantitative approaches, the author proceeds in this paragraph to outline the potential disadvantages of doing this. Sentence 11 explains the practical issues associated with integrating the two approaches (moves 1ci and 1cii). Two key reasons for integrating the two approaches are explained in sentence 12 (moves 1ci and 1cii), while sentence 13 develops this by explaining the circumstances under which the two approaches might be combined: the aims of each method and the nature of the data expected to result are matched. Again, these sentences draw upon 1ci and 1cii moves for justifying the approach in terms of acceptability and previous research. Finally, sentence 15 introduces the reader to the next sub-section on triangulation where the integration of the two approaches is typically encountered.

Again, I would suggest that you cover the analysis in column two of Box 5e below and try to identify the moves that have been used.

Box 5e   Text of methodological approach Section 2

3.2.1 Triangulation

1. As it applies to research, triangulation involves the application and examination of multiple data sources and different data collection methods in the investigation of a single question or phenomenon (Freeman 1998; Patton 1990).

Moves 1bi, 1cii (definition, research)

2. Research can be triangulated on three layers: the level of the data sources; the level of data collection, or research methods; and the level of data analysis (Freeman 1998). 3. In his classic framework, Denzin (1978, quoted in Patton 1990: 187) has outlined four basic types of triangulation:

Moves 1bii, 1cii (description & research)

- data triangulation, using a variety of data;
- investigator triangulation, involving the use of several investigators or researchers;

- theory triangulation, or the employment of more than one perspective to interpret and analyze the data;
- methodological triangulation, involving the use of multiple methods of collecting data.

4. Freeman (1998: 97) has suggested another type of triangulation, triangulation in time and/or location, which entails collecting the same types of data and/or using the same method(s) over a given time period or with the same sources in multiple data-gathering sites.

5. In this study, two key forms of triangulation are applied; namely, 'methodological triangulation' involving the use of multiple tools to collect data (Brown 2001; Patton 1990), and 'time triangulation' whereby multiple data-gathering occasions are used (Freeman 1998). 6. Triangulation can also be achieved by combining qualitative and quantitative methods (Brown 2001; Patton 1990). 7. Hence, it might be deemed a legitimate and effective form of triangulation to combine the qualitative methods of interviews and observations with the quantitative results of questionnaires (Brown 2001).

Moves I bi, I cii
(definition &
research)
Moves I ci, I cii
(acceptability &
research)

8. The use of multiple methods and triangulation in time should enable the investigation of a phenomenon from different perspectives. 9. It should also avoid the vulnerability of any study based on a single method to errors associated with that method (Patton 1990). 10. Furthermore, minimized bias resulting from the utilization of triangulation can contribute to increased confidence in the findings at the stage of data analysis (Freeman 1998).

Move I ci
(acceptability)

Moves I ci, I cii
(acceptability &
research)

11. The process of combining approaches and methods is structured according to the following factors. 12. The first factor involves the relative importance given to each approach within the research study. 13. Quantitative approach is used to facilitate qualitative approach in this study. 14. The second concerns time ordering – the extent to which the methods are carried out consecutively

Move I bii
(description)

Move I bii
(description)

Box 5e (Continued)

or simultaneously (Brannen 1992: 23). 15. Table 5.1 shows that three basic data collection methods – observation, interviews and questionnaires – were employed consecutively for the duration of an entire language course to investigate learners' WTC behavior; questionnaires were collected in the first week, the observation of classes was conducted on a weekly basis, and individual interviews were carried out in the final week.

Move 2b (data collection)

16. In summary, the multiple method strategy was identified as the most appropriate for the present research as it:

Move 1ci (acceptability)

- allowed for thorough analyses of phenomena from different perspectives;
- filled a gap that qualitative research lacked, but which was called for in the previous qualitative studies;
- allowed for the dynamic aspect of time to be examined through time triangulation.

Table 5.1 Matrix of Methodological and Time Triangulation

	Questionnaires	Observations (whole class)	Observations (pair/group)	Individual Interviews
Week 1	✓	✓	✓	
Week 2		✓	✓	
Week 3		✓	✓	
Week 4		✓		✓

Paragraph 1

The first sentence defines the term 'triangulation' (move 1bi), drawing upon two literature sources (move 1cii). This is important when key terms or constructs are introduced for the first time.

Paragraph 2

In this paragraph, the author describes three layers of triangulation (move 1bii) in sentence 2, again drawing upon the available literature (move 1cii). This is followed up in sentences 3 and 4 with a description of the four basic types of triangulation (move 1bii) and further references to the literature (move 1cii).

Paragraph 3

Having defined and described the multi-method approach, the third paragraph goes on to explain what aspects were adopted in the author's research project. Sentence 5 begins with a further description of the two key forms of triangulation employed in the study (move 1bii) and this is supported from the literature (move 1cii). Sentence 6 adds a further defining statement about how triangulation can also be achieved by combining qualitative and quantitative methods (move 1bi) as explained in the literature (move 1cii). The paragraph concludes with a justification of how this might be realized (move 1ci), citing as support the work of Brown (move 1cii). Though not stated explicitly, the implication from these statements is that the study the author is reporting in her thesis adopted these approaches.

Paragraph 4

This paragraph then provides several types of justification for adopting the triangulated approach described in the previous paragraph. In each of the sentences 8–10, the author presents a different advantage for employing the triangulated approach (moves 1ci) and sentences 9 and 10 add further justification in the form of literature support (moves 1cii).

Paragraph 5

The first four sentences of this paragraph describe the factors that were considered when the approaches and methods were combined (moves 1bii). Additionally, sentence 14 defines what is meant by the 'time ordering' factor (move 1bi). At this point, the author introduces the reader to the specific data collection methods that were employed in her study (move 2b) and this is clarified with the tabled representation of the process involved in the three forms of data collection. Sentence 16 concludes this section with a summary of the reasons the triangulated approach was adopted for the study (move 1ci).

Overview of content and structure of this section

Having analyzed this first section of the methodology chapter, we can make a number of overall observations about the content and structure:

1. The author begins with a consideration of the methodology underpinning her study. She explains the basis upon which she determined what methodological approach would be most suitable, citing reasons for adopting an approach that integrated qualitative and quantitative methods. In doing so, she defined these two approaches, stated what their intended purpose was, pointed out the advantages and disadvantages of integration and concluded the first sub-section with a justification for proceeding with an integrated approach in her own study. The second sub-section introduced us to how the two approaches were integrated. The particular way in which she triangulated her data collection sources and methods was defined and described against the background of options she presented in the first part of this sub-section. She then explained how the particular approach would enable her to overcome shortcomings from the adoption of a single approach. Finally, she describes how the combined approaches and the specific methods (questionnaires, interviews and observations) were structured in her study.
2. We can see that the author's focus was almost exclusively on defining, describing and justifying the methodology and methods chosen for the study. To achieve this, we can see (with the exception of 2b moves used in the last paragraph) that move 1 sub-moves were employed.
3. Another noteworthy feature of this section of the chapter is the frequent use of supporting literature (move 1cii) to support the

claims and options presented in the definitions, descriptions and justifications.

4. Having described the methodological options available and having described and justified the methodological approach and the specific methods chosen for her study, the author has set the stage for detailing the specific characteristics of her data collection and analysis.

Data collection procedures

The second discourse move in most research-reporting theses focuses on the various data collection procedures and most often they are presented chronologically according to the sub-move structure given at the beginning of this chapter. The author of our sample thesis begins with a consideration of the participants in her study so we would expect to see a focus on move 2 sub-moves. As you have done before, I would suggest that you read the text given in Box 5f below and try to identify the 2ai–iv sub-moves that have been included.

(a) Participants

Box 5f   Participants

1. The participants (See Table 5.2) were a group of adult learners (n = 10) enrolled in an intensive afternoon General English program at AUT International House in Auckland, New Zealand. 2. These learners (5 males, 5 females) were from a range of LI backgrounds. 3. Among them, four were Chinese, two were Korean, two were from Japan, and two from Switzerland. 4. Five were between 25 and 30 years old, one was over 45 and the rest were under 25. 5. The majority had studied English as a foreign language in their home country for five to eight years; two students however, had had only two years of

Moves 2ai,ii,iii,iv
(location, size,
context,
characteristics)
Move 2aiii
(characteristics)

Box 5f (Continued)

English learning experience. 6. All were classified by their language program as being at intermediate level. 7. Half of them had been in New Zealand for less than 3 months at the time of the study, while one student had lived there for almost a year. 8. Four students had lived in Auckland for six months. 9. The group studied in general English programs at intermediate level in the morning with different groups of students. 10. The afternoon program was basically topic-based and non-assessed, serving the purpose of supplementing the morning program by providing students with opportunities to expand vocabulary and practice macro skills. 11. In-house materials, instead of published course books, were used as the main source of course material. 12. The participants studied in the same afternoon program four afternoons per week from Monday to Thursday for four weeks.

Move 2aiv (context)

Table 5.2 Participant's Background Information

	Gender	Age	Ethnic Group	Mother tongue	Time studying L2	Time in NZ
Ray (S1)	Male	Mid 20s	Japanese	Japanese	5–6 years	1–3 months
Jerry (S2)	Male	Mid 20s	Japanese	Japanese	1–2 years	7–12 months
Sherry (S3)	Female	Mid 20s	Taiwanese	Mandarin	7–8 years	4–6 months
Erica (S4)	Female	Early 20s	Swiss	Swiss-German	5–6 years	1–3 months
Sophie (S5)	Female	Mid 40s	Swiss	Swiss-German	1–2 years	1–3 months
Allan (S6)	Male	Early 20s	Chinese	Mandarin	5–6 years	1–3 months

John (S7)	Male	Late 20s	Chinese	Mandarin	7–8 years	4–6 months
Emily (S8)	Female	Early 20s	Korean	Korean	7–8 years	4–6 months
Cathy (S9)	Female	Mid 20s	Korean	Korean	7–8 years	1–3 months
James (S10)	Male	Early 20s	Chinese	Cantonese	More than 10 years	4–6 months

As you can see, the paragraph has been very clearly organized, beginning in sentence 1 with an overview of all four 2a sub-moves. Sentences 2–7 then detail some of the characteristics of the participants that the author believes the reader should know (move 2aiii): L1 background and gender ratio, age, L2 learning background in home country, language proficiency level and length of time in overseas L2 learning context. This is followed up with an outline of the programme and curriculum of the context in which the study was conducted (moves 2aiv). There are two details that one might also consider including in a sub-section such as the following: (1) providing a heading that includes the word 'context' as well as 'participants' or 'sample' and (2) providing some justification for including the particular sample in the study. Concerning the latter, the reader might also find it useful to know why the particular proficiency level and context were chosen. In other words, sub-move 2e could have been included.

(b) Instruments

In this section, the author introduces us to the three methods employed in her data collection. Rather than detailing the move structure of each of these (observations, interviews and questionnaires), we will focus our attention on one (interviews) because the same structure and considerations apply to the other two methods. The text provided in Box 5g below presents the author's sub-section on interviews. Again, cover column two of the text and try to determine which moves have been employed before reading the analysis.

Box 5g   Interviews

1. Data from classroom observations was supplemented with face-to-face interviews with participants. 2. Interviews are procedures used for gathering oral data in particular categories, as well as for gathering data that was not anticipated at the outset (Brown 2001). 3. Patton (1990) has suggested that the major advantage of using interviews as a data collection tool lies in its strength as a strategy to find out from people things that we cannot directly observe, such as feelings, thoughts and intentions.	Move 2bi (instrument)
	Move 2di (justification)
4. Personal interviews with participants on a one-to-one basis were considered favorable for the study compared to group interviews, since they were more likely to lead to the true views of the respondents when certain levels of confidentiality and trust were required and established (Brown 2001). 5. Furthermore, verbal reports provided by respondents allowed access to unlimited amounts of information and knowledge, characterized by a depth only possible through one-to-one conversation (Marshall and Rossman, 1995).	
6. A standardized structured format was followed in which each participant was asked the same questions. 7. Carefully worded and considered interview questions were written in advance exactly as they were to be asked during the interview (Patton 1990). 8. Each question was checked to ensure that it was free of words, idioms or syntax likely to interfere with the respondents' understanding of them (Glesne and Peshkin 1992). 9. According to Patton (1990: 294), 'standardized interviews must establish a fixed sequence of questions due to their structured format'. 10. The questions regarded as easier to answer appeared at the beginning because answering them would reassure respondents that the questions would be manageable (Glesne and Peshkin 1992).	Move 2bi (instrument)
	Moves 2bi, 2di (instrument & justification)
11. This study also utilized an introspective method known as stimulated recall in the interview process. 12. In second language research, stimulated recall is used to 'prompt participants to recall thoughts	Move 2di (advantage)

they had while performing a task or participating in an event' (Gass and Mackey 2000: 17), or to cause the teacher or the students 'to comment on what was happening at the time that the teaching and learning took place' (Nunan 1992: 94). 13. Stimulated recall is normally carried out with some degree of support, known as stimulus, such as video or audio recordings (Gass and Mackey 2000) or even transcripts of parts of a lesson (Nunan 1992). 14. Because of time constraints, the stimulated-recall approach could not be used in this study in a way that fully exploited its value as a research tool. 15. Thus, participants listened to excerpts only of the audio recordings of their task performance in pairs or groups, and made comments on the pair/group work on or two weeks after the task performance, instead of introspecting about their thoughts at the time of the original interactions.

Move 2bi
(instrument)

Move 2di
(advantage)
Move 2dii
(justification)

16. The interview schedule can be divided into three sections (See Appendix D). 17. The first section consisted of a series of structured questions, originating from the researcher's knowledge of the literature (Glesne and Peshkin 1992). 18. A review of the literature has shown that WTC is influenced by variables such as motivation, level of anxiety and perceived competence. 19. Thus these topics were strategically extracted from studies on communication anxiety (for example, Horwitz et. al. 1986; MacIntyre and Gardner 1994), and motivation (for example, Dörnyei 2002). 20. The second section comprised stimulated recall questions that related to participants' feelings about their task performance in particular groups or pairs. 21. The last section was an additional part which was tailor-made for individual participants whose WTC behavior displayed interesting patterns based on the researcher's observation; for example, participants who demonstrated WTC that was noticeably low or high across the various classroom contexts, and whose WTC participation showed observable changes as the course went by.

Move 2bi
(instrument)

Move 2di
(advantage)

Moves 2bi, 2dii
(instrument &
justification)
Move 2bi
(instrument)

If we consider the whole of this section as one unit rather than as a series of separate paragraphs, we can see that the focus is on describing (move 2bi) one aspect of the data collection process – interviews – and pointing out the functions and advantages of its use (move 2ci). Sometimes, an author will also find it necessary to discuss the disadvantages of using a particular method (move 2ci) so this will typically be presented before or after the advantages. In such cases, move 2cii will follow in order to explain to us the decision(s) that were made in this respect. In our sample thesis, we can see that the author has used move 2cii once to explain how she overcame a particular practical issue (sentence 15).

If we now consider the separate paragraphs of the section, we can see that different aspects of the description of this method are covered:

Paragraph 1

This paragraph begins by reminding the reader that the method to be described (interviews) is one of three methods employed in the study. She proceeds to explain their function and the particular advantage they have over the other methods, signifying therefore their particular contribution to the multi-method approach to data collection in the study (moves 2bi, ci).

Paragraph 2

Paragraph 2 explains why individual interviews rather than group interviews were chosen (move 2di).

Paragraph 3

Here the author focuses on a description of the particular type of interview that was used – the standardized structured format – and in sentences 8–10, she explains why each descriptive detail was important (move 2di).

Paragraph 4

Paragraph 4 explains another feature of the interview type chosen – stimulated recall. Once it has been described (move 2bi), the author explains that a modified version of the typical application was adopted in the study and why this was done (moves 2di, dii).

Paragraph 5

Finally, this paragraph outlines the three sections of the interview schedule and in doing so justifies the specific focus of each section (moves 2di, dii).

Overall, we can see then that this section is concerned primarily with a description of the various components of the method and with an outline of its functions and advantages. The same approach was adopted by our author when introducing the other two methods. In both cases, attention was also given to possible disadvantages of each method. At the end of the Instruments section, the author explains how disadvantages can be overcome by the inclusion of other methods in the multi-method approach.

Having described the three methods that were employed in the data collection of the study, the author turns her attention to a consideration of the extent to which the methods she adopted were valid and reliable. She explains how important data validity and reliability are for the credibility of a study's design, data collection and analysis procedures. Consequently, each is considered in a separate section.

(c) Data reliability

In our sample thesis, the author explains the data reliability measures she undertook in her study. She discusses them with respect to the three data collection methods. We will look at what she says about the interviews only because it is representative of the other two methods. As you read the text below in Box 5h, see if you can identify the move options that have been used.

Box 5h Data reliability measures

1. Reliability provides information about whether the data collection procedure is consistent and accurate (Seliger and Shohamy 1989). 2. To achieve reliability, in the present study, a triangulated approach to data collection was applied in order to enable issues to be examined from a number of perspectives.

Moves
2bii, 2ci
(description &
justification)

3. A structured interview schedule that provided uniform information assured the reliability and comparability of data (Kumar 1996; Newman and Benz 1998), while interviewer effects were minimized by asking the same question of each respondent by the same interviewer (Patton 1990). 4. The stimulus used in this study was audio-tapes of task performance made one or two weeks before the time of the interview. 5. These recorded interviews were transcribed verbatim. 6. Gass and Mackey (2000: 14) have argued that recall would be 95 per cent accurate if the recalls were prompted within 48 hours after the event, but would decline as a function of the intervening time between the event and the recall. 7. Thus it was recognized that the timing of the interviews posed some threat to the reliability of the stimulated/recall part of the interview, so in order to encourage more accurate recall, the researcher provided information concerning the conditions under which the tasks were performed prior to each interview.

8. Assessing the quality of the data collection procedure in the pilot phase allowed the researcher to revise and, where necessary, modify the instruments on the basis of new information, thus improving the reliability of the procedure (Seliger and Shohamy 1989). 9. As Glesne and Peshkin (1992: 30) have suggested, the aim of a pilot study is to learn about the research process, observation techniques, and to get a general sense of the nature of the research setting. 10. Pilot studies should therefore be carried out in situations and with people as close to the realities of the actual study as possible (Glesne and Peshkin 1992).

Throughout this section, you can see that the author has combined a description (move 2bii) and justification (move 2dii) of each aspect. We can also see that each of the three paragraphs focus on a particular issue:

Paragraph 1

This paragraph defines what reliability is and therefore what its function is.

Paragraph 2

As far as one of the three methods (interviews) is concerned, paragraph 2 is about the use of a structured interview schedule as a means of ensuring that reliability was achieved while data were collected from a range of interviewees. The elements of an interview that would ensure reliability are its structured nature and use of the same interviewer. The stimulus material provided on tapes ensured reliability also. Authority was then given to these claims through the use of literature support for the practice.

Paragraph 3

This paragraph mentions the importance of carrying out a pilot study in order to test the instrument. We are introduced to the aim and practical considerations associated with pilot testing.

(d) Data validity

The approach adopted in this section is similar to that in the data reliability section. However, it is interesting that in the author's consideration of the validity of the three methods employed for data collection, discussion was provided on the validity of the questionnaire and observational process but not on the use of the interviews. This is a curious omission. It was probably an oversight. Without this, we will look at what was provided about the validity of the questionnaire. As you read Box 5i below, think about which sentences are providing description and which are offering justification.

Box 5i   Data validity measures

1. Validity is an estimate of the extent to which a study or a set of instruments measures what it purports to measure (Newman and Benz 1998; Seliger and Shohamy 1989). 2. The questionnaire instrument adapted from Hashimoto's (2003) study, which originated from McCroskey and Richmond (1991), was shown to have strong content validity and there was some support for its construct and predictive validity (McCroskey and Richmond 1990, 1991; McCroskey 1992).

> Moves 2bii, 2di (description & justification)

3. However, once the changes were inserted into the questionnaire, a new procedure was created and had to be tested for quality (Seliger and Shohamy 1989). 4. Item analysis was used at the pilot stage, as mentioned earlier in the section, in order to examine the quality of items on the questionnaire as well as to obtain information concerning whether the items were too easy or too difficult, and whether the items were well phrased and easily understood by the respondents (ibid.).

> Move 2bii (description)
> Moves 2bii, 2di, ii (description & justification)

5. Finally, a triangulated approach to the research design and data analysis enhanced the validity of findings. 6. Triangulation at the data collection stage increased the likelihood of measuring what the researcher intended to measure to achieve validity and minimized bias by enabling the researcher to understand the phenomenon from a more holistic point of view (Patton 1990). 7. At the stage of data analysis, the findings resulting from quantitative methods were checked against the findings deriving from qualitative methods (Bryman 1992: 60). 8. In cases where findings conflicted with one another, contradictions were addressed by the researcher in the interpretation of the data and in the linkages made between methods, data and theory (Brannen 1992: 17). 9. In so far as qualitative evidence did not confirm the quantitative results, qualitative evidence was rendered as more trustworthy (Patton

> Move 2bii (description)
> Move 2di (advantage)
> Moves 2bii, 2dii (description & justification)

> 1990) because qualitative research entailed the researcher getting close to the participants and being sensitive to the context and these attributed to greater confidence in the validity of qualitative data over the quantitative (Bryman 1992: 64).

You can see from this analysis that the focus was on describing (all nine sentences except for sentence 6) and justifying the validity measures. The specific content addressed in the section includes (a) an opening definition of validity (sentence 1), (b) how the questionnaire's validity was established (sentences 2–4) and (c) how the use of the triangulated approach enhanced the validity of the study's findings (sentences 5–9). It is also useful to note the specifics included by the author in each of these two main content areas. In discussing how the questionnaire's validity was established, she considered (a) the origin of the questionnaire instrument, (b) the type of validity in question and the extent to which the instrument could be considered a valid measure, (c) the modifications that were made to the original instrument and (d) how the quality of these were then tested. In discussing the contribution of the triangulated approach to the validity of the study's findings, the author justifies its contribution at both the data collection and data analysis stages before explaining how conflicting findings, resulting from the different data sources, were resolved. Throughout the section, strong literature support is offered, giving authority to each of the statements presented. The same approach as that outlined here was taken in the author's outline of issues concerning the validity of the other two methods. Having now described the methods of data collection and the issues surrounding their reliability and validity, the author moves on in the next section to outline the specific steps that were taken in the collection of her data.

(e) Data collection steps

This section of the chapter begins with an overview and a diagrammatical representation of the process.

Table 5.3 Three Stages of Data Collection

Stage 1 Week 1	Stage 2 Week 1–4	Stage 3 Week 4
Self-report questionnaires administered, completed and collected	Entire class observed; pair/group work audio-taped	Volunteer participants (n = 7) interviewed

Each of the three stages identified in Table 5.3 are then described in detail. As you can see from Box 5j below, the author begins with an outline of the steps involved in stages one and two and finishes with her outline of stage three (the interviews). As you read the text, see if you can identify the moves that have been employed.

Box 5j Data collection stage three

1. Stage three of data collection included structured face-to-face interviews (see Appendix D for interview questions) with volunteer participants at the end of the course; that is, in week four, in the classroom where the participants had normally attended the afternoon program.	Move 2c (steps)
2. This allowed more control of the environment in which noises and other distractions were avoided while the interviews were taking place (Brown 2001).	Move 2di,iii (advantage & justification)
3. In order to obtain genuine information more effectively, during the four-week classroom observation, the researcher had made attempts to establish good rapport with the participants (Patton 1990). 4. Furthermore, warm-up questions were asked before each interview to ensure that interviewees felt comfortable and willing to share their views and experiences.	Moves 2c,di (steps & justification)
5. Each interview took between twenty-five minutes to one hour, depending on the amount of detail each participant was ready to provide. 6. Each interview was tape-recorded to ensure the accuracy of data collection.	Move 2c (steps)

---

7. The use of a tape recorder also permitted the researcher to be more attentive to interviewees (Patton 1990).	Moves 2c,diii (steps & justification)

From the analysis, you can see that the author integrates justifications for some of the steps that are presented not only on the basis of the methodology literature but also because of the particular circumstances in which the interviews were being held. In addition to the provision of textual description and explanation, you can further clarify your procedures in the form of diagrammatic representation.

This brings us to the end of the data collection procedures. The next section therefore focuses on how the data were analyzed.

Data analysis

In writing this section of a thesis, you are first going to have to decide the extent to which you are going to provide specific detail and illustrations from the thesis of analytical processes like coding, for example, or whether this level of detail is going to be more helpful for the reader if outlined during the presentation of your findings. While this is not so often a decision that concerns doctoral theses (where such detail is most often provided in a methodology chapter), it is one that should be considered if you are writing a Master's thesis. In our sample thesis, the author has focused on outlining the key steps in the process and left the detail to the presentation of her findings chapter. We are now going to look at the moves she has employed in her outline of the steps that were taken when analyzing the interview data.

Box 5k **Data analysis of interviews**	
I. Data analysis methods used in this study were determined by the research questions driving the study, and the data collection methods used by	Move 3b (justification)

Box 5k   (Continued)

the researcher. 2. Interview data was analyzed qualitatively in order to uncover factors likely to affect learners' willingness to communicate. 3. As a first step, the audiotape recordings of participant interviews were transcribed verbatim. 4. The transcripts were then summarized in the form of matrices (Brown 2001, Marshall and Rossman 1995) to systematically record the categories on the basis of key focusing questions. 5. Content analysis was then used to analyze interview data. 6. Content analysis, as defined by Patton (1990: 381), involves 'identifying, coding, and categorizing the primary patterns in the data', which means analyzing the content of interviews.[2]

Move 3a (steps)

As you can see, apart from the opening sentence which explained the basis on which the data analysis methods were chosen (move 3b), each of the following sentences is simply describing the steps involved (move 3a). You will notice that the author has provided little more than a list of the steps involved in the analysis but it is a clear and useful outline. Once you have read the following chapter in this book on the presentation of findings, you should think about whether or not you agree with the decision that the author took when deciding to present the analytical detail in her findings chapter. This is often the penultimate section of a methodology chapter (assuming all such chapters end with a summary of what has been presented). In this case, however, the author of this thesis has included her outline of ethical considerations between the data analysis and summary sections. While there is no right or wrong place for this discussion, it is often included, as you will have seen from the outline of typical moves given at the beginning of this chapter, in an author's discussion of the sample involved in the research. Wherever you decide to put your discussion of this important information, you need to make sure that it is meaningfully integrated into your argument.

Ethical issues

The focus of any section on ethical issues is on identifying the issues and explaining how they were addressed. As you read the text in Box 5L below, you will see that this is exactly what the author has done. Each of the ten sentences describes how the privacy and confidentiality of the participants were addressed. Essentially, the text outlines the key statements presented in the Information Sheet and Consent Form presented in the appendices. Depending on the specific requirements of your university, you may add to or modify the approach taken here. If you think about the information presented here, you will see that it could well have been presented as one of the 2a sub-moves where the author was describing her sample.

Box 5I   Ethical issues

1. In accordance with the ethical guidelines issued by the university's ethics committees, privacy and confidentiality were respected throughout the research process.

2. The participants were met one day before the study commenced, and the aim of the research and the nature of the study were clearly explained to them. 3. Requests were made for them to participate in the class observations and interviews on a voluntary basis. 4. Requests for pair/group work and interviews to be audio-taped were also made at this point. 5. Participants were assured that participation or non-participation would not in any way affect their grade or relationship with the school. 6. They were provided with copies of Participant Information Sheets (Appendix E) and Consent Forms (Appendix F) on the same day, and were encouraged to take the written forms away with them to think about their willingness to participate in the study.

7. Signed consent was obtained from all participants prior to the commencement of the study. 8. All participants were assigned a number to ensure their identities remained confidential. 9. They were assured that no identifying information would be included in the study. 10. Furthermore, all participants were also assured that the information they provided would be used to fulfill the aims of research only, and were informed of their right to withdraw from the study at any time up until 1 March 2007, without giving a reason.

Summary

The final section of the chapter summarizes the main content areas of the chapter. In some respects, it is a little bit like a shopping list but, if clear cohesive links are made between sentences, it will read more effectively as a summary of the overall argument underpinning the methodological approach of the study. As you read the text in Box 5m below, I would suggest that you do so bearing these things in mind. Think particularly about any places (if at all) where the author could have achieved greater cohesion between one sentence and the next. Finally, ask yourself if you think anything should have been added to the summary.

Box 5m   Chapter summary

1. This chapter has outlined the research design and described the research procedure used in detail. 2. A qualitative approach was adopted in an attempt to fill a gap in the literature that called for verification of self-report WTC by behavioral classroom studies. 3. Moreover, the research design also focused on a triangulated approach to data collection on the basis of methods and time to allow a comprehensive analysis of the research questions, as well as constructing validity and reliability. 4. Classroom observation was selected as the principal tool for gathering data. 5. The data from observations was supplemented by structured personal interviews and use of self-report questionnaire surveys. 6. Self-report questionnaires were intended to capture trait-like WTC, while classroom observation sought to capture actual behavior (state WTC) that was more likely to be affected by external variables. 7. Data validity and reliability were achieved through the adoption of a triangulated approach. 8. Finally, effort was made to ensure the integration of ethical considerations into the research process.

SOME KEY LINGUISTIC FEATURES OF A THESIS METHODOLOGY CHAPTER

In this section, we revisit two of the linguistic features that were considered in earlier chapters – tenses and voice. The importance of choosing the appropriate tense cannot be over-emphasized.

Tenses

The writing of the methodology chapter will involve the use of many tenses: (1) the past simple tense for saying what you did in your study; (2) the present tense for describing the components of the methodology and methods; (3) the present perfect for references to what others have said about the advantages and disadvantages of particular approaches and methods and (4) past perfect for looking back to the time when you carried out a particular procedure or action and for commenting on why you had chosen a particular approach or method. Consider the tenses in the following section (Box 5n) from our sample thesis where the author wrote about the use of interviews in her study.

Box 5n   Tense usage in a methodology chapter

1. Data from classroom observations **was supplemented** with face-to-face interviews with participants. Past perfect
2. Interviews **are** procedures used for gathering oral data in particular categories, as well as for gathering data that was not anticipated at the outset (Brown 2001).
3. Patton (1990) **has suggested** that the major advantage of using interviews as a data collection tool lies in its Present perfect
strength as a strategy to find out from people things that we cannot directly observe, such as feelings, thoughts and intentions.

4. Personal interviews with participants on a one-to-one basis **were considered** favorable for the study compared Past perfect
to group interviews, since they were more likely to lead to the true views of the respondents when certain levels of confidentiality and trust were required and established (Brown 2001). 5. Furthermore, verbal reports provided by respondents **allowed** access to unlimited amounts Past simple
of information and knowledge, characterized by a depth only possible through one-to-one conversation (Marshall and Rossman, 1995).

6. A standardized structured format **was followed** in Past perfect
which each participant was asked the same questions.

Box 5n   (Continued)

7. Carefully worded and considered interview questions **were written** in advance exactly as they were to be asked during the interview (Patton 1990).   Past perfect

8. Each question **was checked** to ensure that it was free of words, idioms or syntax likely to interfere with the respondents' understanding of them (Glesne and Peshkin 1992). 9. According to Patton (1990: 294), 'standardized interviews **must establish** a fixed sequence of questions due to their structured format'. 10. The questions regarded as easier to answer **appeared** at the beginning because answering them would reassure respondents that the questions would be manageable (Glesne and Peshkin 1992).

Past perfect

Present simple

Past simple

Active and passive voice

A combination of active and passive voice structures is usually evident in methodology chapters. As we discussed earlier, students, in some disciplines, are advised not to use the first person singular 'I'. This means that the passive voice tends to be used more often when the object of the sentence rather than the subject is placed before the verb. You can see a number of examples of this in Box 5n above. Consider, for example, sentences 6–8. If the author had used 'I', the active voice would have been used rather than the passive. Arguably, the use of 'I' could become quite tedious for the reader so the use of the passive enables you to avoid this. You may find it useful to discuss this issue with your supervisor.

FREQUENTLY ASKED QUESTIONS

1. What is the difference between 'methodology' and 'methods'?

'Methodology' refers to the theoretical approach or framework that your study was situated in. As such, it will explain the extent to which you employed a quantitative, qualitative and/or multi-method approach. You will need to explain why you chose the approach that was used in your study. This will involve some reference back to the research questions/hypotheses and issues you investigated. You will need to refer to the literature available on research methodology and on research already published in your area of investigation so that you can present an argument for the approach that you adopted for your study.

'Method' refers to the specific methods you employed in your data collection. Thus, you will need to describe the instruments and materials you used and explain why they were appropriate for the research questions/hypotheses you were investigating. The 'methodology' you chose will have informed your choice of 'methods'. In explaining why you chose particular methods, you will need to explain why they were chosen rather than other methods that might have also enabled you to elicit the data you were seeking. Your justification will need to refer to the particular advantages that one method has over another. With any method, there are likely to be shortcomings associated with its use so these need to be acknowledged. Having done that, you need to explain how you sought to overcome these issues. Often, the inclusion of another method or methods within a multi-method approach will have enabled you to address any shortcomings. Inevitably, there will have been some issues that you may not have been able to address, so these need to be acknowledged as limitations. Authors often refer to these in this chapter when talking about the scope or parameters of their study and refer to them again in the concluding chapter.

2. When should the methodology chapter be written?

Most often, authors will have put together an initial draft of their methodology when writing their research proposal and added further detail while carrying out their literature search and, indeed, while doing and reviewing their pilot study. So, this chapter is likely to be a work in progress over many months. Like many students, you may well have kept a diary or log of the various details. If you have done this, the writing process will be a lot quicker and easier. The final draft can usually be written once the data have been analyzed because, at this stage, there is unlikely to be any change to what was done.

FURTHER ACTIVITIES

The following activities could be done individually, in pairs (with another thesis student or with your supervisor) or in small groups:

1. Read the following text (Box 5o) from the questionnaire section of our sample thesis and (1) carry out a move analysis of the text and (2) identify the extent to which different tenses and voice have been used. Consider why the approach has been used and whether or not you think it is rhetorically effective.

Box 5o   Excerpt from questionnaire section

1. Collecting data through the use of a questionnaire has the advantage of ensuring stability of response across a range of questions of interest to researchers. 2. In second language acquisition research, questionnaires are recommended to collect data on phenomena that are not easily observed such as attitudes and motivation (Seliger and Shohamy 1989). 3. As mentioned earlier, a review of the extant literature has revealed that the previous empirical studies carried out on WTC predominantly employed the tool of questionnaire surveys.

4. In this study, self-reported WTC was measured by means of the WTC scale (See Appendix A). 5. The questionnaire used was derived from Hashimoto's (2003) study, developed on the basis of McCroskey and Richmond's operationalisation of the WTC construct, with the underlying assumption that WTC is a 'personality-based, trait-like disposition' (1991: 23). 6. The questionnaire included items related to four communication situations (public speaking, talking in meetings, talking in small groups and talking in dyads) and three types of receivers (strangers, acquaintances, and friends). 7. Eight of the items were distracters in the questionnaire (items 1, 2, 5, 8, 12, 16, 20, 22). 8. The questionnaire was scored on a percentage scale, anchored by 0 being 'never choose to communicate' at one end and 100 being 'always choose to communicate' at the other end. 9. Following McCroskey (1992), the use of the 0–100 probability response

---

> format was chosen over an agree – disagree Likert scale format because it allowed respondents to use a response system commonly adopted in many instructional systems.

2. Choose one of the theses you have included in your literature review or one you can access from your university library and re-read at least one methods section of the methodology chapter and then answer the following questions about its effectiveness:

(a) To what extent was the methodology and the way it was described and justified appropriate for the aims and focus of the study?
(b) Was sufficient justification provided for the methodology and methods? Why or why not?
(c) Were the methodology and the methods sufficiently related to the literature? Why or why not?
(d) Were the methodology and the methods described sufficiently? Why or why not?
(e) What changes would you have made to the reporting of the methodology and methods if it had been your thesis?

3. If you have written a draft of your methodology chapter, you could refer to the move and sub-move options presented earlier in this chapter to evaluate what you have written.

FURTHER READING

If you are interested in reading some of the literature that has informed the material in this chapter, you may find the following references useful:

Bruce, I. (2008). Cognitive genre structures in Methods sections of research articles: A corpus study. *Journal of English for Academic Study,* 7, 38–54.
Dornyei, Z. (2007). *Research Methods in Applied Linguistics.* Oxford: Oxford University Press.

Evans, D., & Gruba, P. (2002). *How to Write a Better Thesis*. Carlton South, Victoria, Australia: Melbourne University Press.

Mackey, A., & Gass, S. (2005). *Second Language Research: Methodology and Design*. Mahwah, NJ: Lawrence Erlbaum Associates.

Paltridge, B., & Starfield, S. (2007). *Thesis and Dissertation Writing in a Second Language: A Handbook for Supervisors*. New York: Routledge.

Rudestam, K., & Newton, R. (2001). *Surviving Your Dissertation: A Comprehensive Guide to Content and Process*. Newbury Park, CA: Sage.

6 Results

INTRODUCTION

This chapter focuses on the presentation of the results/findings of your study. Although some theses combine the presentation of results and the discussion of the results in one chapter, we will be leaving the discussion of results to chapter 7. As we have done with other chapters, we will begin with an outline of the functions of a results chapter before moving on to consider the moves options that might be employed as you think about the content that needs to be presented and how it might be most effectively organized. This will be followed up with an analysis of sections of our sample thesis, an overview of some key presentation and linguistic features of results chapters, a response to frequently asked questions, some further activities and further reading options.

THE FUNCTIONS OF A THESIS RESULTS CHAPTER

The key purpose of this chapter is to present the findings from your investigation in a manner that enables the reader to understand with ease how they address your research questions/hypotheses. In doing so, you will need, at times, to refer back to material presented in your methodology and point the reader forward to what will be considered in the discussion of results chapter. As you present each finding, you will also need to think about whether or not an explanation should be given about what the finding means. Evidence (e.g. statistics, examples, tables or figures) from your data and analysis will feature frequently as you support your findings. Beyond this, you will not need to comment further on the findings in this chapter. In Box 6a below, the various functions are summarized.

Box 6a Functions of a thesis results chapter

1. A presentation of the results/findings of your study that are relevant to your research questions/hypotheses
2. An explanation of what the findings mean (without interpretation)
3. A presentation of evidence in support of your findings
4. References back to details of methodology and background/context
5. References forward to discussion of results issues

THE CONTENT AND STRUCTURE OF A THESIS RESULTS CHAPTER

The macro-structure of the results chapter is most typically organized around the research questions/hypotheses. Sometimes, authors will present their results under thematic or topic headings that are relevant to the research questions/topics. Then again, some authors make use of thematic/topic headings within a research question/hypothesis structure. Having decided on your macro-structure, you will need to decide on the order in which your specific findings will be presented. As you set about introducing each new finding, you will then need to consider what further information should be given to support that finding. As you will see in Box 6b below, there are a number of move options available to you.

Box 6b Move and sub-move options

Moves	Sub-moves
1. Present meta-textual information	a. provide background information
	b. provide references to methodology detail
	c. provide references forward to discussion detail
	d. provide links between sections

---

2. Present results	a. restate research questions/hypotheses
	b. present procedures for generating results
	c. (i) present a result
	c. (ii) provide evidence (statistics; examples; tables; or figures)
	c. (iii) explain what each result means

You may think of other sub-moves that could be added so that the reader is given a full and clear understanding of each result. As we have done in other chapters, we will now consider the ways in which the presentation of results chapter of our sample thesis was presented.

SAMPLE ANALYSIS OF A MASTERS THESIS RESULTS CHAPTER

The author begins her results chapter with a short advance organizer (provided in Box 6c below) to let the reader know how the results will be presented. She explains that the data collected during the research will be presented in a way that enables her to answer the research questions of the study. Then she explains that the results will be presented in two main sections: first the quantitative results derived from (1) the classroom observation and audio-tapes of pair/group work and (2) the questionnaire surveys and then the qualitative results derived from the interviews.

Box 6c   Introduction

An analysis of research data gathered during classroom observation and face-to-face interviews is presented in this chapter, and the research questions posed in Chapter 1 are reiterated and addressed. Quantitative results from the data collected by means of classroom observation and audiotapes of pair/group work, together with self-report questionnaire surveys, are examined, followed by a presentation of the findings from individual, face-to-face interviews with student volunteers. These interviews were carried out on the basis of qualitative content analysis.

This overall structure is a little different to that outlined above but it is, nevertheless, clear and logical. In the discussion of results chapter, the author brings together the various findings from the quantitative and qualitative results in her discussion of each research question. Another approach that could have been used is to present the quantitative and qualitative findings for each research question one after the other. The point to note is the importance of signaling your approach to the reader in the introduction to the chapter.

QUANTITATIVE RESULTS

The quantitative results for each of the research questions are presented in this section.

Research question 1

For the sake of clarity, the findings of this question will be divided into two parts. As you have done in the other chapters, read the first half of the author's text provided in Box 6d below, covering column two, and see if you can identify the move pattern that has been used. Then, we will look at the second half of the text (part B) for this question.

Box 6d   Research question 1 text (part A)

1. This question was directed to an examination of whether learners' self-report of WTC corresponded with their behavior in class in three contexts: in a whole class setting, small groups and pair work.	Move 2a (restate RQ)
2. As a first step, the Spearman rank-order correlation coefficient was used (Brown 1992; Brown 2001) to identify relationships between self-report WTC and WTC in the three classroom contexts: the whole class, small groups and dyads. 3. Each learner's self-report WTC frequency was calculated in terms of a	Move 2b (method)

---

percentage. 4. Thus, raw scores for each individual's participation in the whole class context throughout all observation sessions, as well as in dyads and small groups on the six occasions of task performance were calculated as percentages in order to maintain consistency. 5. Frequency distributions (Coakes and Steed 2003) for each variable (self-report, WTC whole class, WTC pair work and WTC group work) were then computed. 6. Participants were then placed into one of three groups, following an analysis of the distributions for each variable. 7. Students whose frequency score was below 10.0 were classified as low WTC, while those whose frequency scores fell between 10.0 and 15.0 were identified as mid-level WTC. 8. Students whose frequency was above 15.0 were recognized as high WTC.

9. Table 6.1 below illustrates the results of a comparison between self-report WTC and WTC behavior in the three classroom contexts: whole class, dyads and small groups. 10. Each participant's frequency score was included and their WTC level was identified according to criteria based on an analysis of the frequency distributions. 11. WTC whole class refers to frequencies occurring over four weeks. 12. WTC in pair work refers to frequencies occurring on three occasions from Week 1 to Week 3, and WTC in group work includes frequencies occurring on three occasions from Week 1 to Week 3.

Move 2ci,ii (present result; evidence)

Move 2ciii (meaning)

Paragraph 1

You will have noticed that the author begins this section with a restatement of the question being addressed (move 2a) in sentence 1.

Paragraph 2

This paragraph (sentences 2–8) outlines how the data were analyzed and how the results were calculated. In using move 2b throughout the paragraph, you will note that as well as outlining

Table 6.1 Comparisons between Self-report WTC and WTC in Classroom Contexts

Student	Self-report WTC		WTC whole class		WTC in pair work		WTC in group work	
	Frequency (Percentage)	Level	Frequency (Percentage)	Level	Frequency (Percentage)	Level	Frequency (Percentage)	Level
S1	10.0	Mid[b]	11.9	Mid	19.9	High	14.0	Mid
S2	12.0	Mid	13.2	Mid	11.1	Mid	13.5	Mid
S3	6.1	Low	9.6	Low	7.8	Low	8.4	Low
S4[a]	16.5	High	3.6	Low	9.8	Low	6.6	Low
S5	5.6	Low	22.3	High	11.7	Mid	10.9	Mid
S6	15.2	High	9.4	Low	14.1	Mid	18.4	High
S7[a]	15.3	High	5.9	Low	14.2	Mid	12.7	Mid
S9	19.4	High	24.2	High	11.4	Mid	15.4	High

a. Student 4 and Student 7 were absent in Week 4.
b. 'Mid' is short for 'middle'.

these procedures in three steps (step one in sentences 3–4; step two in sentence 5; and step three in sentences 6–8), the author refers to the purpose behind the approach taken (sentence 2). You will also see that she explains/clarifies what was involved in two of the three steps. For step one, sentence 4 explains sentence 3. For step three, sentences 7–8 explain sentence 6. Thus, we not only learn what the procedures were and what their purposes were but also more about how the steps were carried out.

Paragraph 3

Having restated the question and outlined the procedures involved in arriving at the results, we are then presented in paragraph 3 with the results that are relevant to research question 1. This paragraph begins with a tabled representation of the results (moves 2ci and 2cii). In sentences 10–12, the author explains what information is presented in the table. At this point in the text, the table is presented.

The second half of this section (part B) has been further divided into two parts – Box 6e (paragraph 1) and Box 6f (paragraphs 2–4). In Box 6e below, the results that were calculated using the tabled information are presented. Again, you should think about the move patterns incorporated into the text before reading the analysis.

Box 6e   Text of research question 1 (part B, paragraph 1)

13. On the basis of the three groups of participants identified as low, middle and high willingness-to-communicate, the four variables of WTC were analyzed by means of the Spearman rank-order procedure. 14. The mean and standard deviation for each variable, as well as Spearman rank-order correlation coefficients among the variables, were calculated, and the resulting correlation matrix is shown as Table 6.2.	Moves 2ci,b (result; method) Move 2ci (result)

Box 6e   (Continued)

15. From the table, it is clear that relationships among the four variables were statistically significant. 16. Correlation coefficients ranged from 0.5 to −0.866 among self-report WTC, WTC whole class, WTC in pair work and WTC in group work.

Moves 2ci, 2cii
(result; evidence)
Move 2cii
(evidence)

Table 6.2   Correlation Matrix

Variables	Mean	SD	Self-report WTC	WTC whole class	WTC in pair work	WTC in group work
1. Self-report WTC	12.5125	4.98295	1.0			
2. WTC whole class	12.5125	7.31504	−.500	1.0		
3. WTC in pair work	12.5000	3.65279	−.866	.000	1.0	
4. WTC in group work	12.4875	3.79264	.500	−1.000**	.000	1.0

Paragraph 1

The first result to be reported in paragraph 1 of this part is introduced in sentence 13, together with the statistical procedure that was used in the process. Then, in sentence 14, we are referred to Table 6.2 where the specific findings of the investigation are reported. The author also explains that the table reveals the mean, standard deviation and Spearman rank-order correlation coefficients. Sentence 15 explains what these statistics mean in terms of statistical significance and sentence 16 provides the statistical evidence. Thus, this paragraph has (1) introduced a result, (2) explained how it was calculated, (3) presented the statistical findings (with evidence) and (4) commented on its degree of significance.

In paragraphs 2–4 of Box 6f, the specific findings from Table 6.2 are reported. Again, you may like to do your own move analysis of the text first.

Box 6f Research question 1 text (part B, paragraphs 2–4)

17. Self-report WTC correlated significantly and negatively with WTC whole class ($r = -0.5$). 18. Similarly, a strong and negative correlation existed between self-report WTC and WTC in pair work ($r = -0.866$). 19. There was also a significant correlation between self-report WTC and WTC in group work ($r = 0.5$). 20. Self-report WTC appeared to be able to predict WTC in group work; that is, if students reported high willingness-to-communicate in questionnaires, they tended to participate more in group work. 21. In contrast, if self-report WTC appeared to be high, participation in the whole class and pair work was inclined to be low.

Ci,ii (result & evidence)

Ciii (explanation)

22. Correlation among WTC in the three class contexts was found to be less significant. 23. Although a significant correlation was found to exist between WTC in group work and WTC whole class ($r = -1.000$), WTC whole class was not found to correlate with WTC in pair work ($r = 0$). 24. Likewise, WTC in pair work showed no correlation with WTC in group work ($r = 0$). 25. These results suggest that learners' participation in a whole class situation were not consistent with their participation in group work; if, in other words, they appeared to participate actively in a whole class situation, they appeared to be quiet in groups.

Ci,ii (result, evidence)

Ciii (explanation)

26. In summary, the variables of self-report WTC and WTC in various classroom situations were significantly correlated to one another.

- Self-report WTC strongly predicted WTC behavior in group work;
- Self-report WTC negatively predicted WTC in the whole class and pair work;

> **Box 6f   (Continued)**
>
> - There was no correlation between WTC in pair work and WTC whole class or WTC in group work;
> - There was negative correlation between WTC whole class and WTC in group work.

Paragraphs 2–4

In sentences 17–19, the author presents three specific results and evidence from Table 6.2 before explaining in sentences 21–22 what they actually mean. The same pattern occurs in paragraph 3 with sentences 22–24 referring to three more results and evidence before an explanation of their meaning. Paragraph 4 then summarizes the four key results of research question 1. This is a clear and effective move pattern. The summary at the end is particularly helpful for readers who may not have strong statistical knowledge. It is also a means by which you can show your examiner that you fully understand what your results are saying.

Research question 2

The results of investigating this question are also presented in two parts – Box 6g (paragraphs 1–3) and Box 6h (paragraphs 4–5).

> **Box 6g   Text of research question 2 (Part A)**
>
> 1. This question considered whether learners' WTC behavior in class differed according to three different contexts: the whole class, small groups and pair work.   Move 2a (restate research question)
>
> 2. The question was analyzed using ANOVA with an F-test in order to assess the statistical significance of the resulting difference among the three groups of data – whole class, small groups and dyads.   Move 2b (method)

3. The means and standard deviations of WTC across the three class contexts are presented in Table 6.3. 4. The analysis of variance (ANOVA) revealed no results for F-test and significance (see Table 6.4). 5. This was because the means for WTC in each context were nearly identical. 6. As shown in Table 6.3, for whole class was 12.5125, for pair work was 12.5000 and for group work was 12.4875.

Moves ci,ii
(results & evidence)

Moves ciii,ii
(explanation & evidence)

Table 6.3   Summary of Mean and SD for WTC in Classroom Contexts

	Whole class	Pair work	Group work
Mean	12.5125	12.5000	12.4875
SD	7.31504	3.65279	3.79264

Table 6.4   Summary of Results of ANOVA for WTC in Classroom Contexts

		Sum of Squares	df	Mean Square	F	Sig.
Whole class	Between Groups	374.569	7	53.510		
	Within Groups	.000	0			
	Total	374.569	7			
Pair work	Between Groups	93.400	7	13.343		
	Within Groups	.000	0			
	Total	93.400	7			
Group work	Between Groups	100.689	7	14.384		
	Within Groups	.000	0			
	Total	100.689	7			

Paragraphs 1–3

As was the case with research question 1, we again see in sentence one that the author has restated the research question and followed this up with a statement about how the question was investigated (sentence 2). In paragraph 3, two results are presented with tabled evidence (sentences 3 and 4), an explanation of what they mean (sentence 5) and with supporting evidence (sentence 6).

Part B (paragraphs 4–5) then considers the specific findings for each finding.

Box 6h   Text of research question 2 (Part B)

7. In order to consider this question, however, it was necessary to look at each learner's participation[4] in each situation. 8. The results of each learner's WTC behaviors in three classroom contexts – whole class, dyads and small groups – during the course are accordingly summarized in Table 6.5, and presented graphically as Figure 6.1.

Moves ci,ii
(result &
evidence)

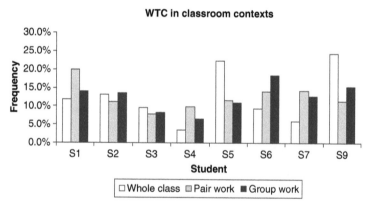

Figure 6.1   WTC in Classroom Contexts
Note: mean score for each context was 12.5%.

9. An ANOVA F-test revealed no differences among the three classroom contexts. 10. However, differing patterns emerged in examining individual learners' WTC behaviour in each context. 11. From Figure 6.2, it is apparent that Student 5 and Student 9 demonstrated similar patterns in terms of their WTC behaviour in the whole class, compared with their WTC in pair and group work. 12. Their combined whole class WTC exceeded 45%, which accounted for just less than half of the participation of the entire 13. In contrast to this high participation in the whole class, their participation in pair and group work was

Move ci (result)
Moves cii,iii
(evidence &
explanation)

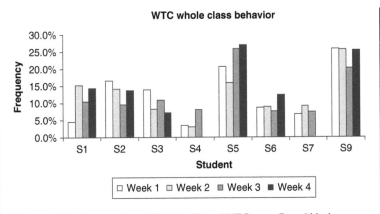

Figure 6.2 Frequencies of Whole Class WTC over Four Weeks

Note: 1. Student 4 and Student 7 were absent in Week Four.
2. Mean score for whole class was 12.5%.

much lower. 14. Their whole class WTC frequency was almost twice that of pair/group work. 15. Student 6 and Student 7 displayed differing patterns, since their participation in whole class was considerably less than that in pair and group work. 16. Student 2 and Student 3 maintained undeviating WTC behaviors across the three situations. 17. Student 4, as discussed in 4.1.1, remained very quiet in all three contexts. 18. She appeared, however, to participate most actively in pair work, whereas her whole class WTC was extremely low. 19. Likewise, Student 1's WTC in pair work was highest compared to his WTC in other two situations. 20. The total of his participation in each situation was, however, substantially greater than that of Student 4.

Paragraph 4

This paragraph begins by stating that it is necessary to now examine the individual learner's participation. The findings are presented in Table 6.5 above and in Figure 6.1 above. You can see that the use of a Figure makes the tabled results so much more accessible for the reader. Figures are particularly helpful if there is a lot of statistical information in a table on a particular finding.

Table 6.5 WTC in Classroom Contexts

Student	WTC whole class		WTC in pair work		WTC in group work	
	Sum	Frequency (%)	Sum	Frequency (%)	Sum	Frequency (%)
S1	189	11.9	219	19.9	133	14.0
S2	209	13.2	122	11.1	128	13.5
S3	152	9.6	86	7.8	80	8.4
S4	57	3.6	108	9.8	63	6.6
S5	353	22.3	129	11.7	104	10.9
S6	149	9.4	156	14.1	175	18.4
S7	93	5.9	157	14.2	121	12.7
S9	383	24.2	126	11.4	146	15.4
Mean		12.5		12.5		12.5
SD		7.32		3.65		3.79

Paragraph 5

Evidence and explanation of the various individual learner's behaviour are considered in this paragraph. Another Figure (6.2 above) is presented in order to clearly reveal the patterns. Note how the author brings together similar patterns in her explanation of the evidence (e.g. the similar patterns of students 5 and 9; the differing patterns of students 6 and 7). In this paragraph, the author is drawing the reader's attention to the patterns but is not interpreting them or explaining why they might have occurred: this will be the focus of the discussion of results chapter.

At this point in our analysis of the results chapter from our sample thesis, we will turn our attention to what the author presented in her qualitative results section rather than present the findings of research question 3. This is because a similar pattern was employed in the presentation of results.

Qualitative results

The qualitative results from the interviews that were conducted with the participants during the last week of their study programme are presented in four sections: (1) responses to general questions, (2) responses to stimulated-recall questions, (3) individual

Table 6.6 Summary of Self-report Details from Part I Interview

	Reasons for studying L2	Self-assessed L2 proficiency	Personality	Self-perceived communication competence
Ray (S1)	To get a better job; to communicate with people from other countries	– Overall average. – Have no confidence in speaking.	– Generally quiet.	– Competent – All the classmates were friends, so he could speak easily.
Jerry (S2)	To make friends	– Overall very poor. – Speaking very poor.	– Not too quiet or too talkative. – Talk more with flat mates; quiet when unable to explain something in L2; not quiet when speaking in L1.	– Not competent. – He perceived his L2 as being poor and was disappointed when he was not understood by others.
Sherry (S3)	To get a better job	– Overall poor. – Speaking and pronunciation poor.	– Quiet compared with talkative classmates. – She could talk a lot when she knew about the topic.	– Not competent. – But she would not hesitate to ask questions and would be happy to provide answers she knew.
Erica (S4)	For jobs and holidays	– Overall average. – Speaking average.	– Generally quiet. – She only talks when she feels good with people and situations.	– Competent.

Table 6.6 (Continued)

	Reasons for studying L2	Self-assessed L2 proficiency	Personality	Self-perceived communication competence
Sophie (S5)	For traveling	– Overall between good and average. – Speaking below average.	– Generally extroverted and talkative. – Talk with everybody outside the classroom; inside the class, it depends on the topic.	– Competent.
Allan (S6)	To get a good job	– Overall average. – Speaking has improved.	– Not talkative. – Talk more with friends, but not much with strangers.	– Not competent. – He found it difficult to ask questions. But if someone asked questions first, he would answer.
Cathy (S9)	For traveling	– Overall average. – Speaking used to be poor.	– A talkative person. – Talk with friends and family members; when strangers initiate communication, she talked to them.	– Competent for most of the time. – When she did not know the words in L2, she did not regard herself as competent.

questions and (4) factors affecting WTC behaviour in class. We will look at a selective sample of the different types of reporting given in the chapter.

Responses to general questions

The questions in the first part of the interview sought, by means of self-report responses, to uncover factors likely to affect WTC. The detailed responses elicited from the interviews with each participant, were summarized by the author and reported in two tables, the first of which (presented below in Table 6.6) covered four of the eight questions that were asked.

Table 6.6 reports the responses from the first four questions that were asked of each participant: (1) their reasons for studying English as a second language; (2) their self-assessed proficiency level in English; (3) how they characterized their personality and (4) their self-perceptions of their communicative competence. The author has presented their responses in summarized note form and has used the same terms of reference for responses that were offered more than once. For example, the second question records responses in overall terms and categorizes the responses as average, poor and good. Consistency of reporting in this manner makes it possible for frequencies of a particular response to be calculated.

Using the tabled information, the author then provides a textual report on each of the eight questions. The approach that was taken was similar for each question so we will focus our attention on only one of these questions. Box 6i below presents the textual report on question 1 about the participants' reasons for studying English as a second language.

Box 6i   Text of responses to question 1 – reasons for studying L2

1. Data from the interviews revealed that the participants were predominantly learning English for pragmatic reasons such as job hunting and traveling. 2. Comments from individual participants, concerning perceptions of their personality, suggested that most regarded themselves as

---

Box 6i   (Continued)

being generally quiet, while a relatively small number thought they were talkative and extroverted. 3. Their self-rated L2 proficiency was generally consistent with self-perceived communication competence; that is, those who thought that their L2 proficiency was average overall regarded themselves being competent in L2 communication, and conversely, those who regarded their L2 proficiency as being poor also thought they were not competent in L2 communication. 4. All participants appeared to be relaxed in the language class, a view supported by the participants themselves who, in most cases, commented that they felt relaxed in the class. 5. Their favorite class organization appeared to be a small class, made up of groups each containing three or four people.

In this paragraph, the author presents a series of separate findings in response to the question about reasons for studying English as a second language and in each case reveals the extent to which each type of response was offered. Rather than provide specific frequency counts, the author uses words such as 'predominantly' (sentence 1), 'generally' (sentences 2 & 3) or 'all' (sentence 4). Had there been more interviewees in the study, numerical counts would have been worth doing. In this study, the author was focusing on categories of response.

Responses to stimulated-recall questions

The second part of the interview (stimulated-recall) asked participants to comment on either the pair work or group work they engaged in. The responses that were provided are summarized in Table 6.7 below.

The textual report on these findings (see Box 6j below) begin with a summary of the detail that was elicited and this is followed up with an analysis of the responses about pair work (see Box 6k below).

Table 6.7 Summary of Self-report Details from Part II Stimulated-recall Interview

	Tasks used for stimulated-recall	Comments on pair/group work	Comments on tasks
Jerry (S2)	– Pair work. – Open, one-way[6] tasks. – Comparing and sharing personal experiences.	– Enjoyed discussion in both pairs. – Erica was a new student and he did not talk much with her in Task 1. – James was his friend with whom he felt more relaxed talking in Task 2.	– Both topics were difficult.
Sherry (S3)	– Pair work. – Task 1 was open, one-way task and involved comparing the sharing personal experiences. – Task 2 was a closed, one-way, and text-base reading comprehension task.	– Enjoyed working with Cathy who was quite friendly in Task 1. – Sophie talked for most of the time as she had some ideas in Task 2.	– Had few ideas about both topics. – Task 1 (Week 1) was funny. – Task 2 (Week 2) was not so interesting.
Erica (S4)	– Group work. – Open, two-way and divergent tasks (role plays).	– Group Work 1 not very good; nobody talked much. – Group Work 2 was better.	– Had no ideas about what to say. – Task 1 (Week 2) not interesting; learnt little and had few chances to use new structures and vocabulary. – Task 2 (Week 3) was better; had to use past tense and knew what to do.
Sophie (S5)	– Group work. – Open, two-way and divergent tasks (role plays).	– Felt happy in all groups. – Liked both groups.	– Disliked role plays. – Preferred Task 2 (Week 3); knew about the film and could tell the stories; had little to say in Task 1 (Week 2).

Table 6.7 (Continued)

	Tasks used for stimulated-recall	Comments on pair/group work	Comments on tasks
Allan (S6)	– Pair work. – Open, one-way tasks. – Comparing and sharing personal experiences.	– Sophie talked and extended the topic in Task 1. – Talked more in Task 2.	– Task 1 (Week 1) not interesting. – Had no idea what to talk about in Task 2 (Week 3).
Cathy (S9)	– Group work. – Task 1 (Week 1) involved listing and ranking items. Task 2 (Week 2) was open, two-way and divergent.	– Always enjoyed discussions and tried to participate. – Difficult to compare group work.	– Any task was OK; she wanted to learn L2. – Task 1 was fun.

Box 6j   Textual summary of overall findings

1. Table 6.7 represents a summary of self-report details of stimulated-recall interview. 2. Most of the interviewees showed increased participation in either pair work or group work later in the course than at the beginning of the course. 3. The exceptions were Erica and Sophie who seemed to be quiet during group work in both weeks, though each expressed a preference for the second group work session. 4. Factors that appeared to affect their participation were the interlocutor(s) they worked with, knowledge about topics being discussed, and preference for task types.

Two key findings emerged from the tabled responses are as follows: (1) increased participation and (2) a range of factors determined participation. The specific responses of participants to their pair work and group work involvement are then analyzed. Our attention will focus on what the author presented in her textual analysis of pair work responses (see Box 6k below).

Box 6k   Textual responses to questions about pair work

1. Jerry, Sherry and Allan were each asked to recall their performance in pair work. Jerry, when asked to compare two tasks he performed in pairs in Week 1 and Week 3 – both of which were of the same task type (comparing and sharing personal differences) but on different topics – reported that both were difficult for him, and as a consequence, he found it difficult to contribute much because he lacked knowledge of the topic. 2. To the different partners he worked with during each task, he explained that because Erica (in Week 1) was a new student, he did not talk much with her. 3. On the other hand, he reported feeling far more relaxed talking with James (in Week 3), who was his friend and in front of whom he was not afraid of making mistakes. 4. This probably explained why he talked significantly more in Task 2 than in Task 1[7].

5. Allan was asked to comment on the same tasks. 6. Like Jerry, he also worked with different partners in each task. 7. He had similar problems with both tasks, and felt that he had little to contribute, although he found

---

Box 6k   (Continued)

Task 2 more enjoyable than Task 1. 8. He remembered that his partner, Sophie, tried to extend the topic when he talked very little in Task 1, but he participated more in the discussion for Task 2 when working with Erica. 9. However, reasons for his increased participation were not provided.

10. Sherry was requested to comment on the same tasks from Week 1 and Week 3. 11. Her response was similar to that of the previous two students who expressed concern about lacking knowledge of the topic under discussion, and how this inhibited her use of L2. 12. Her personal preference was Task 1 which she regarded as more interesting. 13. This was probably because she was able to relate herself to the topic, which was about mischievous behaviors in childhood. 14. Questioned about how she felt about the pair work, Sherry said she enjoyed working in Task 1 with Cathy who was friendly and seemed to have many ideas; and Sophie, with whom she worked in Task 2, and who contributed to most of the conversation.

The responses of three participants to pair work are presented here. Each was asked to reflect upon their performance during the different tasks they performed. The author begins by analyzing Jerry's explanations for his performance. Allan's and Sherry's responses on the same tasks were then noted. Points of similarity are highlighted. For example, in paragraph 2 the similar experiences of Allan and Jerry are recorded and in paragraph 3, it is noted that Sherry's response was similar to that noted by Allan and Jerry. Thus, while presenting the responses of participants separately, the author draws the reader's attention to where similarities and differences exist. Further comment on these details emerges in the discussion chapter. Here, the responses are simply presented and the patterns between responses noted.

Factors affecting WTC behaviour in class

This section introduces us to another form of reporting the interviewees' responses: the use of verbatim quotes from the interviews.

In this section of her qualitative results, the author refers to eight factors from the interview data that might affect WTC behaviour in class. In each case, the same approach is taken to the way each factor is presented so we will focus our attention on one of these: the number of interlocutors involved in the communication (see Box 6L).

Box 6I Textual responses to factors affecting WTC behaviour in class

1. A number of factors likely to influence WTC behavior in classroom contexts were identified from the interview data. 2. For example, the number of interlocutors in a particular context appeared to affect participants' WTC in class, with the majority of participants reporting that a small number of interlocutors involved in communication, was preferable, the ideal number suggested being three or four. 3. According to Sophie:

'I think when you work in a pair you don't speak a long time. But in a group, you have three of four people. I think in a group is good' (Transcripts 03/02/2005).

4. Jerry provided more detail in support of his preference for group work:

5. 'Group, three or four is good for me . . . Some people talking about, some people listen, and then sometime I'm helping, talking about. Sometime help each other' (Transcripts 02/02/2005).

The overall finding is presented in sentence 2 and this is followed up in sentences 3 and 5 with direct quotations from the transcribed interviews in order to illustrate the views that were expressed. As evidence of the fact that the view was held by more than one participant, two quotations are presented. There is no need to provide any more unless further insights are revealed.

The chapter then ends with a short summary, similar to those we have already examined in earlier chapters.

SOME KEY LINGUISTIC AND PRESENTATION FEATURES OF A THESIS RESULTS CHAPTER

Tenses

As we have seen in earlier chapters, the tenses and voice (active v passive) selected for the results chapter also depends on the function of the statement being made. It is interesting to note some differences for the reporting of quantitative and qualitative results. Consider, first of all, the italicized verbs in Box 6m (an example of quantitative reporting).

Box 6m   Tense usage in the reporting of quantitative results

1. This question *considered* whether learners' WTC behavior in class differed according to three different contexts: the whole class, small groups and pair work.
   Past simple

2. The question *was analyzed* using ANOVA with an F-test in order to assess the statistical significance of the resulting difference among the three groups of data – whole class, small groups and dyads.
   Passive – past

3. The means and standard deviations of WTC across the three class contexts *are presented* in Table 6.3.
   Passive – present

4. The analysis of variance (ANOVA) *revealed* no results for F-test and significance (see Table 6.4).
   Passive – present

5. This *was* because the means for WTC in each context *were* nearly identical. 6. As shown in Table 6.3, for whole class *was* 12.5125, for pair work *was* 12.5000 and for group work *was* 12.4875.
   Past simple

In sentence 1, the past simple tense is being used to report a completed action in the past. In sentence 2, the passive voice is used to reverse the subject–object focus of the sentence and the past tense is used because a completed activity is being referred to. Again the passive voice is being used in sentence 3 to place the focus on the two types of results rather than on the table. Here, the present tense is being used because the table is present and is to be looked at here and now. The past simple tense is used in sentences 5 and 6 because the author chose to focus on the fact that the events informing the results occurred in the past. It would be equally acceptable for the author to have used the present tense because the statistical reasons being offered can be seen in the tabled results presented here. Thus, there are sometimes options in the tense or voice that is used but on each occasion there will be a functional reason for the choice that is made.

By contrast, it is interesting to note the consistent use of the past simple tense in the reporting of the qualitative results in Box 6n below.

Box 6n   Simple past tense in reporting quantitative results

1. Data from the interviews *revealed* that the participants were predominantly learning English for pragmatic reasons such as job hunting and traveling. 2. Comments from individual participants, concerning perceptions of their personality, *suggested* that most regarded themselves as being generally quiet, while a relatively small number *thought* they were talkative and extroverted. 3. Their self-rated L2 proficiency *was* generally consistent with self-perceived communication competence; that is, those who *thought* that their L2 proficiency was average overall *regarded* themselves being competent in L2 communication, and conversely, those who *regarded* their L2 proficiency as being poor also *thought* they *were* not competent in L2 communication. 4. All participants *appeared* to be relaxed in the language class, a view *supported* by the participants themselves who, in most cases, *commented* that they *felt* relaxed in the class. 5. Their favorite class organization *appeared* to be a small class, made up of groups each containing three or four people.

Hedging

It is also noteworthy that the author in her qualitative reporting makes extensive use of hedging. This is understandable given the limited number of items being referred to in the responses

169

of the small number of participants. Because frequencies are not calculated, the author, nevertheless, attempts to draw our attention to where patterns of similarity and difference exist and, in doing so, moderates her observations in case further research of a quantitative nature reveals that the observations are not generalizable. The italicized adjectives, verbs and adverbs in Box 60 reveal the extent to which hedging has occurred.

Box 60   Tense usage in the reporting of qualitative results

1. Data from the interviews revealed that the participants were *predominantly* learning English for pragmatic reasons such as job hunting and traveling. 2. Comments from individual participants, concerning perceptions of their personality, *suggested* that most regarded themselves as being *generally* quiet, while a *relatively* small number thought they were talkative and extroverted. 3. Their self-rated L2 proficiency was *generally* consistent with self-perceived communication competence; that is, those who thought that their L2 proficiency was average overall regarded themselves being competent in L2 communication, and conversely, those who regarded their L2 proficiency as being poor also thought they were not competent in L2 communication. 4. All participants *appeared* to be relaxed in the language class, a view supported by the participants themselves who, *in most cases*, commented that they felt relaxed in the class. 5. Their favorite class organization *appeared to be* a small class, made up of groups each containing three or four people.

Presenting quantitative results visually

There is much that can be said about the use of tables and figures, and even more that can be said about those that are created to reveal the findings of particular types of statistical testing. However, it is not the aim of this book to provide that type of detailed information. There are plenty of books available that you can consult for this level of detail. One that is particularly helpful for new researchers and first-time thesis writers is that by Rudestam and Newton (see further reading section below for citation details). The aim of this section is to introduce you to some general guidelines for the visual representation of your results.

1. There are different opinions about whether to compare values down columns or across rows. The key point to remember is consistency in approach throughout your thesis. Your supervisor will be able to help you make a decision about which approach is appropriate for the kind of information you want to present.
2. Avoid any attempt to put every detail from your computer print-out in a table. Be selective so that the focus is clear for your reader. Visual appeal and clarity are key considerations. Do not be afraid to permit white space.
3. A clear relationship between tables, figures and text is essential. Your text must make use of the table and figure information. There must be a clear connection between what is presented in your table and what you present in a figure. The relationship must be represented in both the structure of the table and the use of language. For example, if you are referring to a particular measure or scale with a particular designation, the same designation must be used in all tables, figures and text.
4. Use appropriate labels for each form of visual representation and make sure they are not too long. Avoid abbreviations unless they have been clearly introduced in preceding text or are supplied in notes at the foot of the visual representation.
5. Consult the most recent style manual used in your discipline for guidelines on the key components of a table and figure: numbering, titles, headings, body and notes.

Presenting qualitative results

Compared with the presentation of numbers and statistics in quantitative research, qualitative research is more likely to present words and ideas. Consequently, there is likely to be more flexibility with the format you choose for presenting your findings. Qualitative data from interviews, focus groups, field notes and the like needs to be summarized and this is often done by developing categories or codes. As we have seen in our sample thesis, the author managed to effectively present her summarized detail in tables where the findings of the participants were grouped according to the specific questions that were asked. Thus, the interview questions became the categories. In other data, thematic categories can be similarly developed. Once this has been achieved, you can then discuss each category and illustrate it in your textual presentation with examples from your tables and with direct quotations from your transcribed records.

FREQUENTLY ASKED QUESTIONS

1. Do I need to present all the results from my analyzed data?

The short answer to this question is no. If the results of your analysis contribute to the answering of a research question/hypothesis, you should present these results. It may also be the case that your analysis reveals some interesting or significant findings that are not related to a question/hypothesis that you set out to investigate. In such cases, it may be worth including a question or subsidiary question in the design of your study. Before doing this, however, you should discuss the idea with your supervisor.

2. Which of my results should be visually represented?

If you only have a few statistics to report, it is usually unnecessary to present them in a table. For example, if you are only reporting on the difference between two means, it would be just as clear to convey the difference in a textual statement. However, if you are presenting the findings of a question that involved the comparison of mean scores for a number of variables, it would be clearer if the statistics were presented in a table. If you have a range of variables and test types presented in a table, it may then be helpful for the reader if you present the statistics in a figure (e.g. graph, diagram, chart etc). Thus, the more detailed and complex your findings are, the more difficulty the reader will experience when reading this information for the first time. To assist with this process, visual representations can be very helpful. However, do not get carried away with the use of figures for all tables. This could have the reverse effect, namely, cluttering the page and making the presentation difficult to navigate through.

3. How much explanation should accompany tables and figures?

Because you have presented the detail in a table or figure, there is no need to describe each detail in the accompanying text. Your text should focus on the key observations and patterns revealed in the table or figure and explain in non-technical terms what they mean, that is, as a finding that contributes to the answering of a research question/hypothesis. The explanation should be as concise as possible, yet extensive enough to convey clearly the range of detail that you consider important.

FURTHER ACTIVITIES

The following activities could be done individually, in pairs (with another thesis student or with your supervisor) or in small groups:

1. Read the following text from our sample Masters thesis and analyze the move structure used by the author.

I. This question considered whether an individual learner's WTC behavior in class changed over time; in the case of this study, a one-month language program. 2. The question was addressed by examining each participant's whole class behavior for each week in an effort to identify changes in WTC, and whether observed changes represented trends of any kind. 3. Pair work behavior and group work behavior over the first three weeks were also investigated. 4. Because it was difficult to examine changes in WTC behavior by considering the class as a whole (since mean scores for WTC frequencies in each week were identical), the results in each context were interpreted on the basis of individual learners.

5. Table 6.6 and Figure 6.2 present the results of frequencies of whole class WTC behavior in each week of the course. 6. The frequencies are presented as percentages as well as in raw scores. 7. From Table 6.6 it is apparent that Student 5 and Student 9 maintained the highest

(Continued)

percentage levels of participation in the whole class, although their WTC frequencies reveal different patterns of change during the four weeks of observation. 8. Student 5's WTC score decreased from 20.6% to 15.9% and then increased considerably to 25.9% and remained nearly the same in the next two weeks. 9. Student 9's WTC frequencies, on the other hand, remained close to 25.0% for three weeks, although the score dropped to 20.3% in Week 3.

2. Read the following table from research question 3 of our sample thesis and write a suitable text to accompany the table.

Table 6.8 Frequencies of WTC in Pair Work over Three Weeks

Student	Week 1 Sum Frequency (%)	Week 2 Sum Frequency (%)	Week 3 Sum Frequency (%)	3 Weeks Sum Frequency (%)
S1	59 (18.6)	95 (25.4)	65 (15.8)	219 (19.9)
S2	21 (6.6)	35 (9.4)	66 (16.0)	122 (11.1)
S3	21 (6.6)	43 (11.5)	22 (5.3)	86 (7.8)
S4	21 (6.6)	27 (7.2)	60 (14.6)	108 (9.8)
S5	56 (17.7)	41 (11.0)	32 (7.8)	129 (11.7)
S6	53 (16.7)	34 (9.1)	69 (16.7)	156 (14.1)
S7	55 (17.4)	46 (12.3)	56 (13.6)	157 (14.2)
S9	31 (9.8)	53 (14.2)	42 (10.2)	126 (11.4)
Mean	12.5	12.5	12.5	12.5
SD	5.56	5.63	4.24	3.65

3. Create a graph to visually represent the frequencies of students 1–4 from Table 6.8 above.
4. If you have written a draft of your results chapter, you could refer to the move and sub-move options presented earlier in this chapter to evaluate what you have written.
5. Read the following table (Table 6.9) from our sample thesis and write a suitable text on one of the four themes/questions to accompany the table. You may like to ask a fellow student or your supervisor for feedback on your text.

Table 6.9 Summary of Self-report Details from Part I Interview

	Feelings towards the learning environment	Motivation to study in this program	Language class anxiety	Favorite class organization for communication
Ray (S1)	– Very relaxed in class. – Liked learning together with the class who were very friendly and kind.	– Motivated to learn L2. – Motivation went down in Week 3 because he had already read the book *Rain Man*.	– Not confident when speaking incorrect L2. – Not appropriate to volunteer answers when not called upon in his home culture. – Not afraid of making mistakes.	– Preferred group of three or four; more people involved; conversation became funnier. – Pair work too casual; only heard opinions from one person. – Disliked whole class; aware of being regarded by peers as talkative or wanting teacher's attention.
Jerry (S2)	– Very relaxed in class. – Liked classmates very much.	– Not motivated. – Programmes boring; too much writing; topics difficult to discuss. – Studied for attendance.	– Not confident when speaking in L2. – Not afraid of making mistakes in class but afraid of NS not being able to understand him outside class. – Wanted to be corrected by teacher.	– Group work preferred; more people involved in talking, listening and helping one another. – Quality of pair work depends on partner's personality. – Embarrassed to make mistakes in whole class.
Sherry (S3)	– Relaxed in class. – Liked this class; they were quite friendly.	– Motivated – Learnt from this course and improved L2.	– Not confident when speaking in L2. – Acceptable to make mistakes.	– Not preference.

Table 6.9 (Continued)

	Feelings towards the learning environment	Motivation to study in this program	Language class anxiety	Favorite class organization for communication
Erica (S4)	– Relaxed in class. – Not so good because she did not learn much and she did not know the class.	– Motivated, – Paid for the course. – Wanted to learn.	– Not confident sometimes. – Not afraid of making mistakes.	– Pair work preferred; could speak more and consult partner. – Group work funnier. – Unhappy with whole class; felt inhibited to talk in front of quick responders.
Sophie (S5)	– Very relaxed in class. – Enjoyed learning with the classmates and the teacher; it was great fun.	– Motivated to learn and to improve speaking in particular.	– Generally confident when speaking in L2 in class. – Wanted to be corrected.	– Preferred group work; more people involved; could learn more. – Whole class OK. – Could not talk long in pairs.
Allan (S6)	– Relaxed in class. – Enjoyed studying with the class. – But he preferred a smaller class size.	– Motivated to improve L2 skills and to use L2.	– Not afraid of making mistakes. – Wanted to be corrected by teacher to improved L2.	– Favorite was small groups; could benefit from members whose L2 was better. – Not many chances to talk to classmates when teacher talked in whole class. – Pair work involved only one partner.
Cathy (S9)	– Very relaxed and comfortable in class. – Enjoyed learning with the class; she had a good time.	– Motivated to communicate and speak with other classmates.	– Not confident when she could not understand what teacher said. – Acceptable to make mistakes in the learning process.	– Whole class preferred; could hear opinions from all. – Pair work not good; only listened to one person.

FURTHER READING

If you are interested in reading some of the literature that has informed the material in this chapter, you may find the following references useful:

Brett, P. (1994). A genre analysis of the results sections of sociology articles. *English for Specific Purposes, 13,* 47–59.

Cooley, L., & Lewkowicz, J. (2003). *Dissertation Writing in Practice: Turning Ideas into Text.* Hong Kong: Hong Kong University Press.

Evans, D., & Gruba, P. (2002). *How to Write a Better Thesis.* Carlton South, Victoria, Australia: Melbourne University Press.

Paltridge, B., & Starfield, S. (2007). *Thesis and Dissertation Writing in a Second Language: A Handbook for Supervisors.* New York: Routledge.

Rudestam, K., & Newton, R. (2001). *Surviving Your Dissertation: A Comprehensive Guide to Content and Process.* Newbury Park, CA: Sage.

Yang, R., & Allison, D. (2003). Research articles in Applied Linguistics: Moving from results to conclusions. *English for Specific Purposes, 33,* 365–385.

7 Discussion of Results

INTRODUCTION

In this chapter, we will be considering the discussion of results as a separate chapter from the presentation of results and conclusion chapters. Some theses combine their presentation and discussion of results or findings in a single chapter. For example, this is sometimes the pattern for theses or dissertations at Masters level. In contrast, some theses combine the discussion of results and conclusion in one chapter. The approach that is taken is often determined by disciplinary preference and the type of thesis that is being written. A discussion with your supervisor will assist you in arriving at the option best suited to the research you are reporting. The approach taken in this chapter can be easily adapted to the choice you make. If you decide to combine your presentation of results with your discussion of those results, you will most likely divide your results into meaningful sections (e.g. according to research questions/hypotheses, thematic or methodological foci) and present your discussion of each section of results immediately after each section or part section of results that has been presented. The same approach would apply if you decided to combine your discussion of results and your conclusion. Considering now the discussion of results as a single chapter, we begin with a consideration of the purpose and functions of the chapter before looking at a range of move and sub-move options that might be considered. The chapter will again conclude with a discussion of some key linguistic features of discussion chapters, some answers to frequently asked questions, further activities and suggestions for further reading.

THE FUNCTIONS OF A THESIS DISCUSSION OF RESULTS

The key purpose of this chapter is to discuss the meaning and significance of the results or findings of the research you are reporting. Consequently, the discussion will have a number of functions, including, for example, those presented in Box 7a below.

Box 7a   Functions of a thesis discussion of results

1. An overview of the aims of the research that refers to the research questions or hypotheses
2. A summary of the theoretical and research contexts of the study
3. A summary of the methodological approach for investigating the research questions or hypotheses
4. A discussion of the contribution you believe your results or findings have made to the research questions or hypotheses and therefore to existing theory, research and practice (i.e. their importance and significance)
5. This discussion will often include an interpretation of your results, a comparison with other research, an explanation of why the results occurred as they did and an evaluation of their contribution to the field of knowledge

---

If you are combining your conclusion with your discussion, the additional functions of the chapter would probably include those referred to in the next chapter of this book.

As the next section shows, these functions may be realized through a series of move and sub-move options.

THE CONTENT AND STRUCTURE OF A THESIS DISCUSSION OF RESULTS

For each section of results you present, the following moves and sub-moves in Box 7b can be useful.

Box 7b   Move and sub-move options

Moves	Sub-moves
1. Provide background information	a. restatement of aims, research questions and hypotheses b. restatement of key published research c. restatement of research/methodological approach
2. Present a statement of result (SOR)	a. restatement of a key result b. expanded statement about a key result
3. Evaluate/comment on results or findings	a. explanation of result – suggest reasons for result b. (un)expected result – comment on whether it was an expected or unexpected result c. reference to previous research – compare result with previously published research d. exemplification – provide examples of result e. deduction or claim – make a more general claim arising from the result, for example, drawing a conclusion or stating a hypothesis f. support from previous research – quote previous research to support the claim being made g. recommendation – make suggestion for future research h. justification for further research – explain why further research is recommended

---

These moves and sub-moves provide you with a number of options to consider when deciding how you will discuss your results. They should not be seen as a prescriptive list of moves/sub-moves or as a list of moves that should be presented in this order. The extent to which our sample thesis has employed these options and recycled them is the focus of our next section.

SAMPLE ANALYSIS OF A MASTERS THESIS DISCUSSION OF RESULTS

The author of our sample thesis discusses her results in four sections with each focusing on one of the four research questions that guided the study. In this section, we will consider the moves and sub-moves that she used in her discussion of research questions 1 and 4. The approach taken for research questions 2 and 3 is the same so will not be presented. Before we look at the first research question, we will note in Box 7c what has been included in the introduction to the chapter.

Box 7c   Introduction to Discussion of Results

This chapter provides a detailed analysis of key research findings presented in chapter 4, with reference to each of the research questions. The results of the study are also discussed in relation to previous research studies. The first section (Section 5.2) discusses the relationship between self-report WTC and WTC behavior in the three classroom contexts observed. Differences observed in WTC behavior in each of the contexts, and variations in WTC over time, are discussed in Sections 5.3 and 5.4. The fourth section presents the factors that learners perceived as being of most importance in affecting their WTC in class. The last section is a brief summary of the chapter.

Like previous chapter introductions, this one also provides an advance organizer of what is to be presented in the chapter. The author begins by explaining that her discussion will be organized around the four research questions and that it will focus on the relationship between her results and those of earlier research studies. While this is an important feature of a discussion chapter, it should also refer to the other features of the discussion that are included in the discussion chapter (e.g. the sub-moves in Box 7b above that have been used in the text). The paragraph then outlines the focus of each section of the discussion chapter.

Research question I

Before reading the move and sub-move analysis in column two of Box 7d below, you may like to cover it first and carry out your own analysis.

> ### Box 7d   Text of first research question discussion
>
> | | |
> |---|---|
> | 1. The first research question investigated the relationship between self-report WTC and WTC behavior in class. 2. This question relates to the concept of WTC as a trait variable or a state variable. | Move 1a (background) |
> | 3. Correlation analysis[8], indicated that self-report WTC strongly predicted WTC behavior in group work, while self-report WTC negatively predicted WTC in the whole class and pair work. 4. The strong positive relationship between self-report WTC and WTC group work demonstrated that participants' self-report WTC was consistent with their WTC behavior in group work. 5. However, participants' WTC behavior in the whole class and in pair work contradicted their WTC reported in the questionnaire. | Move 2a (SOR)

Move 2b (expansion) |
> | 6. Results from an examination of the relationship between self-report WTC and WTC behavior in three classroom contexts on an individual basis, were found to be mixed (see Table 4.1). 7. For half of the class (Sherry, Jerry, Ray and Cathy), self-report WTC was consistent with actual WTC behavior in class, whereas for the other half (Erica, Sophie, Allan and John), self-report WTC contradicted classroom WTC behavior. | Move 2a (SOR)

Move 2b (expansion) |
> | 8. It is interesting to note that Erica, who reported high WTC in the questionnaire, | |

appeared to demonstrate low WTC across the three class situations, as well as appearing to lack interest in class. 9. She was observed to be rather quiet and worked on the tasks by herself most of the time. 10. Sometimes the teacher had to call her to participate in classroom activities or call on her to answer questions. 11. In the interview, she attributed her extremely low participation across all contexts to the classmates whom she seemed to be unfamiliar with, and some of whom, to her, seemed to have 'snatched' opportunities for communication. 12. For this learner, WTC did indeed appear to be influenced by lack of familiarity with interlocutors and lack of appropriate opportunities to participate in class.

Move 3d (illustration)

Move 3a (explanation)

13. Likewise, Allan and John, who reported high WTC, seemed to be relatively quiet in the classroom. 14. Both demonstrated low willingness to communicate, particularly in the whole class situations. 15. This may have been due to an over-optimistic self-reporting of their WTC, suggesting, perhaps, that their self-reported WTC was in effect paying 'lip service' to the survey, without actually having made any commitment to participate actively (Dörnyei and Kormos 2000: 290). 16. In other words, they may have been concerned about presenting themselves favorably, thus causing them to respond inaccurately. 17. Another possible interpretation could be that they had high trait WTC, but they may have needed extra encouragement from the teacher, and more cooperation from their peer classmates, for them to participate more. 18. Allan actually expressed his concern in the interview that there were not many chances to talk when the teacher talked most of the time in the whole class situation.

Move 3d (illustration)

Move 3a (explanation)
Move 3c (previous research)

Move 3a (explanation)

19. Sophie, who belonged to the group of low WTC in self-report, on the other hand, showed very high WTC in the whole class and was an equally active participant in pair and

Box 7d (Continued)

group work. 20. Her self-report WTC seemed to contradict her claim of herself being generally an extroverted and talkative person, a personality trait which was manifested in her actual behavior in class.

Move 3d (illustration)

21. The findings above seemed to reveal the dual characteristics of WTC proposed in previous studies: the trait-like WTC and the situation-based WTC. 22. MacIntyre et al.'s (1998: 546) claim that WTC in L2 should not be limited to a trait-like variable but a 'situational variable with both transient and enduring influences' appeared to be supported by the findings of this study.

Move 3e (claim)

Move 3c (previous research)

23. It is possible, however, that learners' WTC behavior in the class context was influenced by both trait-level WTC and state-level WTC. 24. As MacIntyre et al. (1999) has pointed out, trait WTC may bring an individual into situations in which communication was likely, but once in a particular situation, state WTC could influence whether communication would take place. 25. MacIntyre and his colleagues argued that state WTC predicted and affected the decision to initiate communication within a particular situation, which may explain the discrepancy between self-report WTC and WTC class behavior among half of the participants in the present study. 26. Although their trait-level WTC determined their general tendency in communication, state-level WTC appeared to have a particularly strong impact on the participants' communication behavior in particular class contexts. 27. Their state-level WTC seemed to be influenced by a variety of factors, which will be discussed in Section 5.5.

Move 3e (claim)

Move 3f (previous research)

Move 3e (claim)

28. The findings of the relationship between self-report WTC and WTC behavior in class in this study do not appear to fully support those of Chan and McCroskey (1987), in which observational data indicated that fewer of the students

Move 3b (unexpected)

who had low scores on the WTC scale participated in class, than those who scored high on the scale. 29. In Chan and McCroskey's study, more of the total participation in class came from students with high scores than from students with low scores. 30. They therefore concluded that class participation may be in large measure a function of an individual's orientation toward communication (trait WTC), rather than a situation-specific response (state WTC). 31. The results of the current study do not support this conclusion. 32. A possible explanation is that Chan and McCroskey considered students' participation in class where L1 instead of L2 was used. 33. This would make the findings of the present study not comparable with those of Chan and McCroskey's, since WTC in L2 was unlikely to be 'a simple manifestation of WTC in the L1' (MacIntyre et al. 1998: 546). 34. It was also possible that not all learners with high WTC in the present study exhibited high participation. 35. Similar results to those of Chan and McCroskey may have been found had the sample size been larger.

Move 3c (previous research)

Move 3a (explanation)

36. The findings of the present study do, however, support Weaver's (2004) conclusion that students' WTC within the EFL classroom varied significantly across different speaking situations and tasks.

Move 3b (expected) Move 3c (previous research)

37. The findings also lend support to MacIntyre et al.'s (2001a: 377) acknowledgement of the weakness of the self-report questionnaire as a reliable method for examining state WTC, because 'thinking about communicating in the L2 is different from actually doing it'. 38. While their study failed to find any evidence for the existence of state WTC by using the single method of a self-report survey, in the present study, state WTC was identified by observation of WTC in three classroom contexts. 39. On this basis, structured observation is proposed as a more suitable method for the examination of state WTC, a variable difficult to identify by using a single self-report technique.

Move 3b (expected) Move 3c (previous research)

Move 3g & h (further research & justification)

Although we can see a recycling of moves in this discussion of question 1, there is, nevertheless, a very clear organizational pattern throughout the text:

1. A restatement of the question being addressed (sentences 1–2).
2. A statement of result is presented with a short expansion (sentences 3–7).
3. Illustrations of the statement of result are then presented, first those revealing the same pattern – Erica (sentences 8–12) and Allan and John (sentences 13–18) – and then an illustration of the opposite pattern – Sophie (sentences 19–20).
4. In presenting the first group of illustrations, explanations are also offered. Previous research was referred to once in order to support the explanation being given.
5. As a result of these illustrations of the statement of result, further claims are made (sentences 21–27) and these are supported with reference to previous research.
6. The extent to which the results were expected or unexpected in light of previous research is then considered (sentences 28–38). First the author considers the research that her results do not support (sentences 28–35) and, in doing so, offers some explanations (sentences 32–35). Then she refers to studies that do support her results (sentences 36–38).
7. The discussion closes with a recommendation and justification for further research (sentence 39).
8. The author then moves on to discuss her results for the second research question. However, we will focus our attention now on part of her discussion of the results for research question 4.

Research question 4

Research question 4 investigated the factors that could have an influence on willingness to communicate behaviour in class. In a separate sub-section for each factor, the author considers a range of variables. These are identified in her introduction to the discussion of question 4 results (see Box 7e below). Once we have looked at this introduction, we will focus our attention on her discussion of two of these factors (medium of communication and cultural influences).

Box 7e   Introduction to research question 4

1. Previous studies have found that factors such as motivation, attitudes, perceived competence and language anxiety played a role in determining willingness to communicate and actual communicative behavior. 2. Cultural context was also confirmed by empirical studies as having an impact on the relationship between WTC and its antecedents. 3. These factors were identified by means of self-report data. 4. This study, however, managed to distinguish a number of factors that appeared to affect learners' WTC in various class situations from both self-report data and learners' perceptions from the participant interviews.

5. These factors included: number of interlocutor(s) in a particular context, familiarity with interlocutor(s), interlocutor(s)' task performance, familiarity with and interest in topics under discussion in tasks, task types for pair/group work, medium of communication and participants' cultural backgrounds.

This introduction begins with the claim that self-report data have already revealed some factors that can determine a learner's willingness to communicate. However, the author explains that her study, drawing upon wider data sources, uncovered additional factors. Each is then listed prior to being discussed in detail in separate sub-sections.

We shall now analyze how the author went about discussing her results on factor 5 – the influence of the medium of communication on a learner's willingness to communicate. Again, you may like to do your own analysis first.

Box 7f   Text of factor 5: Medium of communication

1. Whether L1 or L2 was used as the medium of communication also appeared to exert an influence on learners' WTC. 2. As MacIntyre et al. (1998: 546) have suggested, the differences between L1 and L2 WTC may be due to 'the	Move 2a (SOR) Move 3a (explanation)

Box 7f (Continued)

uncertainty inherent in L2 use', and the level of linguistic competency can be one differentiating factor existing in LI and L2 WTC. 3. In this study, Jerry noted that a lack of linguistic competence in L2 inhibited communication, but when LI was used, such a problem was not present. 4. Cathy also considered a lack of lexical resources in L2 as a factor affecting her perceived competence, which in turn influenced willingness to communicate at times. 5. This seems to support House's (2004) claim that lack of actual linguistic competence in L2 can prevent communication.

Move 3d
(exemplification)

Moves 3b & c
(expected result
& previous
research)

6. Differences in LI and L2 WTC were also detected in task engagement in pair work. 7. Dörnyei and Kormos (2000) found that learners' relationships with their interlocutor had a considerable impact on the extent of their engagement in the task in LI, but this relationship failed to emerge in an L2 task. 8. They suggested that when L2 was used as the medium of communication, the challenge of trying to express one's thoughts using a limited linguistic code in addition to decoding the interlocutor's utterances, created an emotional state different from the communication mode in LI, which may 'alter one's perceptions of the constraints of the interaction' (ibid. 293). 9. Differences in WTC in pair work in both LI and L2 were, however, beyond the scope of this study and were not, as a consequence, examined. 10. It appears to be another area for further research.

Move 2a
(SOR)
Move 3c
(previous
research)

Moves 3a & c
(explanation &
previous
research)

Move 3g
(further
research)

As we saw in the analysis of the discussion of research question 1 results, this discussion of one factor that emerged in the results of research question 4 also revealed a cyclic pattern of moves in response to a statement of result. Explanation, previous research and exemplification moves were the most frequently employed. Arising from the discussion, the author identifies a further area for research.

We shall now analyze how the author presented her results on factor 6 – cultural influences on a willingness to communicate.

Box 7g Text of factor 6: Cultural influences

1. Kubota has argued that 'the way people think, speak, write and behave is certainly influenced by the culture in which they are brought up, and certainly cultural difference indeed exists' (1999: 15).	Move 1b (background)
2. As discussed in the previous chapter, empirical studies have shown that the cultural context has an impact on WTC, and WTC varies greatly across cultures. 3. Although these studies were associated with WTC in LI, it seemed one's cultural background also exercised an effect on one's WTC in L2.	Move 2a (SOR)
4. At least one learner voiced this point of view in this study.	Move 3d (exemplification)
5. Ray mentioned the influence of his home culture on his willingness to communicate and relatively low level of communication in whole class situations. 6. Ray came from Japan, a country whose culture in its discourse is characterized by collectivism, which promotes conformity to group goals and homogeneity, the opposite face of which is the discouragement of individual diversity and creativity (Kubota 1999: 20; Cheng 2000).	Move 3c (previous research)
7. Cultural norms in Japan do not value talkativeness, and Japanese generally tend not to be outspoken (McCroskey et al. 1985). 8. It has been cited in the literature that this perceived reticence was due to Confucian influences (Cheng 2000).	Moves 3a & c (explanation & previous research)
9. Ray attributed his relative quietness in the whole class to this cultural influence rooted deeply in him. 10. He regarded it as inappropriate to volunteer answers without being called upon by the teacher.	Move 3d (exemplification)
11. This attitude seems to support Tsui's (1996) claim that there appeared to be a widespread phenomenon in Hong Kong schools that students would not take the initiative to volunteer answers until they were called upon by the teacher to do so.	Moves 3b & c (expected & previous research)

Box 7g   (Continued)

12. It was an interesting point that Ray made of himself, of not wanting to be regarded as being talkative or attracting the teacher's attention by his peers. 13. He seemed to be aware of his relations with others in the social process of conducting himself (Wen and Clément 2003) as he tried to avoid negative evaluation from his peers (Tsui 1996). 14. This concern he felt about the judgment of the peers upon his WTC behavior in class caused him to become less likely to get involved in whole class communications.

Moves 3a & d (explanation & exemplification)

Moves 3a,c,d (explanation, previous research, exemplification)
Moves 3a & d (explanation & exemplification)

15. Although for particular learners such as Ray, WTC seemed to reflect the influence of his home culture, it was not possible to draw any pattern between cultural background and WTC behavior in class in this study, given the small sample size; and it was not a research question addressed in this study.

Moves 3e & g (implied hypothesis for further research)

Again we can see the cyclic nature of the move structure of this discussion of cultural influence on willingness to communicate. This is particularly the case with respect to explanations (sentences 7, 8, 12, 13, 14) and references to previous research (sentences 6, 7, 8, 13) that support the key exemplification (Ray in sentences 5, 6, 9, 10, 12, 13, 14) of the statement of result (sentence 3).

Unlike the analyses of research questions 1 and 4 (medium of communication), the discussion of cultural influences begins with some literature-based background claims (sentences 1–2) before introducing the statement of result in sentence 3.

The author ends this sub-section of her discussion with an implied hypothesis that might be tested in further research (sentence 15). The hypothesis arises out of the preceding discussion but for which her data was too limited for any firm claim or conclusion to be made about the influence of cultural background on willingness to communicate behaviour in class.

Conclusion

The text in Box 7h below presents the author's summary of her discussion.

Box 7h   Conclusion

1. This chapter has summarized the present study's findings, and discussed them with reference to each of the research questions. 2. The results have also been considered in relation to relevant previous studies.

3. The study confirmed that WTC in L2 possesses dual characteristics: a trait-level WTC and a state-level WTC. 4. It suggested that trait WTC may determine an individual's general tendency to initiate communication, but it was state WTC that predicts whether communication would take place. 5. Being a situational-based variable, WTC in L2 was found to be subject to change across situations and over time.

6. It supported the claim that a single self-report method was not appropriate to examine state WTC, a variable detected by the observational method employed in this study. 7. Structured classroom observation was thus proposed to be a more suitable method for the examination of state WTC in class, a variable difficult to identify by using a single self-report method.

8. Results from this study pointed to a number of factors that participants perceived as being of most importance in influencing their WTC behavior in three classroom contexts. 9. These factors included: number of interlocutor(s) in a particular communicative context, familiarity with interlocutor(s), interlocutor(s)' task performance, self-confidence in communication, familiarity with and interest in topics under discussion, task types for pair/group work, medium of communication and influence of participants' cultural backgrounds.

The section begins with a restatement of how the findings have been discussed in relation to the 4 research questions and previous research. Paragraph 2 summarizes the key findings and comments on their significance. Paragraph 3 explains how the discussion has also focused on the importance of examining WTC by means of structured classroom observation rather than by means of the previously employed single self-report method. Paragraph 4 summarizes the discussion of factors that might influence a learner's willingness to communicate in class. The summary has therefore drawn our attention to the key contribution that the study has made to existing knowledge (theory, research and practice). The significance of the findings and this discussion will be highlighted in the conclusions that the author offers in her concluding chapter.

SOME KEY LINGUISTIC FEATURES OF A THESIS DISCUSSION OF RESULTS

As you discuss the significance of your findings in light of the big picture (the literature you presented in your literature review chapter), there will occasions when you can be quite assertive about the significance and contribution of your findings to the field you are working within and occasions when you need to be more tentative in the claims that you make. While care needs to be taken, you should not shy away from claiming that a particular finding supports or does not support existing research and knowledge if it does. In the discussion chapter, you will seek to account for particular findings. If you are presenting possibilities rather than absolute certainties, you need to make sure that you hedge in your presentation of them. In the previous chapter, we referred to various ways in which hedging can be achieved. As an example of how this can be achieved in the discussion chapter, consider the extensive use of hedging approaches that have been used in the following paragraph (Box 7i) from our sample thesis discussion.

Box 7i   Hedging in the discussion of results

1. The findings above **seemed** to reveal the dual characteristics of WTC proposed in previous studies: the trait-like WTC and the situation-based WTC. 2. MacIntyre et al.'s (1998: 546) claim that WTC in L2 should not be limited to a trait-like variable but a 'situational variable with both transient and enduring influences' **appeared** to be supported by the findings of this study. 3. It is **possible**, however, that learners' WTC behavior

Hedge verb

Hedge verb
Adjective

---

in the class context was influenced by both trait-level WTC and state-level WTC. 4. As MacIntyre et al. (1999) has pointed out, trait WTC *may* bring an individual into situations in which communication was likely, but once in a particular situation, state WTC *could* influence whether communication would take place. 5. MacIntyre and his colleagues argued that state WTC predicted and affected the decision to initiate communication within a particular situation, which *may* explain the discrepancy between self-report WTC and WTC class behavior among half of the participants in the present study. 6. Although their trait-level WTC determined their general tendency in communication, state-level WTC *appeared* to have a particularly strong impact on the participants' communication behavior in particular class contexts. 7. Their state-level WTC *seemed* to be influenced by a variety of factors, which will be discussed in Section 5.5.

Modal verb — (line: trait WTC *may*)
Modal verb — (line: state WTC *could*)
Modal verb — (line: which *may*)
Hedge verb — (line: *appeared*)
Hedge verb — (line: *seemed*)

In another example from our sample thesis, consider the author's willingness to be up front and assertive in sentence 3 below.

Box 7j   Assertiveness in the discussion of results

1. In Chan and McCroskey's study, more of the total participation in class came from students with high scores than from students with low scores. 2. They therefore concluded that class participation may be in large measure a function of an individual's orientation toward communication (trait WTC), rather than a situation-specific response (state WTC). 3. The results of the current study *do not support* this conclusion. 4. A possible explanation is that Chan and McCroskey considered students' participation in class where L1 instead of L2 was used.

FREQUENTLY ASKED QUESTIONS

1. Can I introduce any new literature in the discussion of results?

The short answer is no. It is sometimes the case that your data analysis will reveal something interesting or important that you had not previously considered so you may need to find out what literature exists on the issue. Having done that, you should include it in your literature review so that you can refer back to it in your discussion chapter.

2. How much of the literature review do I need to refer to when comparing one of my results with that of a study referred to in the literature review?

You should only refer to the relevant part of the study presented in the literature review. For example, if you are comparing findings, you should only refer to that finding and not other details that may have been presented in your review of the study. For a clear example of how this can be done, see the approach that the author took in Box 7j above. On other occasions, you may want to compare an aspect of the methodology of your study (e.g. sample size, setting) and that of another study referred to in the literature review. Again, only the relevant aspect of the methodology should be discussed.

3. To what extent do the ideas presented in the discussion chapter have to be based on the literature presented in the literature review?

The reasoning that you offer in support of a claim or the reasoning that you offer as an explanation for a result, be it expected or unexpected, should be informed by the literature. Your own ideas, outside the literature, should only be used to argue a point that is based on the literature.

FURTHER ACTIVITIES

The following activities could be done individually, in pairs (with another thesis student or with your supervisor) or in small groups:

1. Read the following text from our sample thesis where the author is discussing her results on the influence of the medium of communication on a learner's willingness to communicate and identify the moves that have been employed.

1. Whether LI or L2 was used as the medium of communication also appeared to exert an influence on learners' WTC. 2. As MacIntyre et al. (1998: 546) have suggested, the differences between LI and L2 WTC may be due to 'the uncertainty inherent in L2 use', and the level of linguistic competency can be one differentiating factor existing in LI and L2 WTC. 3. In this study, Jerry noted that a lack of linguistic competence in L2 inhibited communication, but when LI was used, such a problem was not present. 4. Cathy also considered a lack of lexical resources in L2 as a factor affecting her perceived competence, which in turn influenced willingness to communicate at times. 5. This seems to support House's (2004) claim that lack of actual linguistic competence in L2 can prevent communication. 6. Differences in LI and L2 WTC were also detected in task engagement in pair work. 7. Dörnyei and Kormos (2000) found that learners' relationships with their interlocutor had a considerable impact on the extent of their engagement in the task in LI, but this relationship failed to emerge in an L2 task. 8. They suggested that when L2 was used as the medium of communication, the challenge of trying to express one's thoughts using a limited linguistic code in addition to decoding the interlocutor's utterances, created an emotional state different from the communication mode in LI, which may 'alter one's perceptions of the constraints of the interaction' (ibid. 293). 9. Differences in WTC in pair work in both LI and L2 were, however, beyond the scope of this study and were not, as a consequence, examined. 10. It appears to be another area for further research.

2. Read the above text again and evaluate the stance taken by the author as you consider the extent to which her statements are hedged.
3. Referring to one of the theses or dissertations you reviewed in your literature review or one that you obtained from your library to do some of the further activities suggested in earlier chapters of this book, you may like to evaluate it in light of the move and sub-move options presented earlier in this chapter.
4. If you have written a draft of your discussion of results chapter, you could refer to the move and sub-move options presented earlier in this chapter to evaluate what you have written.

FURTHER READING

If you are interested in reading some of the literature that has informed the material in this chapter, you may find the following references useful:

Basturkmen, H., & Bitchener, J. (2005). The text and beyond: Exploring the expectations of the academic community for the discussion of results section in Masters theses. *New Zealand Studies in Applied Linguistics, 11*, 1–19.

Bitchener, J., & Basturkmen, H. (2006). Perceptions of the difficulties of postgraduate L2 thesis students writing the discussion of results section. *Journal of English for Academic Purposes, 5*, 4–18.

Cooley, L., & Lewkowicz, J. (2003). *Dissertation Writing in Practice: Turning Ideas into Text.* Hong Kong: Hong Kong University Press.

Dudley-Evans, T. (1986). Genre analysis: An investigation of the introduction and discussion sections of MSc dissertations. In M. Coulthard (Ed.), *Talking about Text.* Birmingham, UK: University of Birmingham.

Dudley-Evans, T. (1998). Genre analysis: An approach to text analysis for ESP. In M. Coulthard (Ed.), *Advances in Written Text Analysis* (pp. 219–228) London: Routledge.

Evans, D., & Gruba, P. (2002). *How to Write a Better Thesis.* Carlton South, Victoria, Australia: Melbourne University Press.

Hopkins, A., & Dudley-Evans, T. (1988). A genre-based investigation of the discussion section in articles and dissertations. *English for Specific Purposes, 7*, 113–122.

Hyland, K. (2005). Stance and engagement: A model of interaction in academic discourse. *Discourse Studies, 7*, 173–192.

Paltridge, B., & Starfield, S. (2007). *Thesis and Dissertation Writing in a Second Language: A Handbook for Supervisors.* New York: Routledge.

Rudestam, K., & Newton, R. (2001). *Surviving Your Dissertation: A Comprehensive Guide to Content and Process.* Newbury Park, CA: Sage.

8 Conclusion

INTRODUCTION

The conclusion of a thesis is often presented in a separate chapter but sometimes it may be combined with the discussion of results. Conventions may vary not only from discipline to discipline but also within disciplines. Therefore, it would be wise for you to consider the options outlined in this chapter in relation to other theses you have read in your discipline area, and to discuss the approach you are thinking of adopting with your supervisor.

Although the concluding chapter or section of a thesis may vary in focus and rhetorical structure with other theses, all theses will have the same over-riding aims or purpose, namely, to explain what the study has aimed to achieve, what it has achieved and what importance and significance the achievements have for theory, research and practice. The following functions of a conclusion will enable you to think about what specific content might be included and about how it might be most effectively organized. Again, the chapter will close with some key linguistic considerations, frequently asked questions, further activities and suggestions for further reading.

THE FUNCTIONS OF A THESIS CONCLUSION

The following functions in Box 8a are typically characteristic of thesis conclusions but the extent to which each is focused on will vary according to the conventions of the discipline, the nature of the research aims, methodology and results of your study.

Box 8a   Functions of a thesis conclusion

1. A reminder of the aims (e.g. research questions/hypotheses) and key methodological features of your study
2. A summary of the findings of the study
3. An evaluation of the importance and significance of your study with commentary on (a) its contribution to the development of theory and research and (b) any limitations
4. Practical applications
5. Recommendations for further research

How these functions are realized in a conclusion is our focus in the next section.

THE CONTENT AND STRUCTURE OF A THESIS CONCLUSION

The following move options in Box 8b reflect the functions identified above:

Box 8b   Move and sub-move options

Moves	Sub-moves
1. Restatement of aims and methodological approach of study	a. restatement of aims of study (research questions/hypotheses) b. restatement of key features of research methodology & methods
2. Summary of findings	a. summary of key findings
3. Evaluation of study's contribution	a. significance of findings (for theory & research development) b. significance of findings for practical application

---

a. justification for 3a & 3b
b. identification of any limitations

4. Recommendations
   for further research

a. recommendations for further research
b. justification for 4a

Most empirically based theses will present a conclusion that draws upon at least three of these four moves. Moves 1 and 2 are sometimes combined as one move. In her introduction to the chapter, the author of our sample thesis outlines the four headings under which she presents her conclusions.

SAMPLE ANALYSIS OF A MASTERS THESIS CONCLUSION

As with the previous chapters, we will examine the extent to which our sample thesis conclusion has made use of the move and submove options identified above. But first of all, it is worth noting in Box 8c below how the author introduced her final chapter.

Box 8c   Introduction

1. This chapter presents, firstly, a summary of the key findings of the research, followed by a consideration of pedagogical implications for teachers and institutions, as well as recommending implications for further research. 2. The limitations of the study are assessed subsequently. 3. The chapter concludes with a brief summary of the preceding sections.

As an advance organizer, this is a very clear listing of the areas that will be included. This said, the first area – a summary of key findings – is presented.

Summary of key findings

Referring to the moves and sub-moves presented in Box 8d above, you may like to cover column two of the text below and undertake your own move analysis of this section.

Box 8d   Text of summary of key findings

1. The primary objective of this study was to investigate the relationship between self-report WTC and WTC behavior in a second language classroom; and in particular, to examine whether WTC should be regarded as a trait variable or a state variable. 2. The secondary aim of the study was to examine how WTC varied across three classroom contexts: whole class, groups and dyads, within the one-month time period of a language program.

Move 1a
(aims)

3. The study was carried out at a university language center in Auckland, in an intermediate language classroom. 4. A triangulated approach was adopted in order to collect data by means of multiple instruments – structured classroom observation, participant interviews and self-report WTC questionnaires over the period of the language course.

Move 1b
(method)

5. Although quantitative analyses of data indicated some relationships, these relationships could not be generalized beyond the specific learners and contexts involved in the present study.

Move 3d
(limitation)

6. A preliminary finding from this research was that the willingness to communicate construct in a second language was identified to be both a trait-like variable and a state variable. 7. The role of trait WTC appeared to determine a general tendency to communicate, whereas state WTC predicted whether communication in a particular situation would take place. 8. As a situational variable, WTC was found to be a complex and dynamic variable subject to change over time. 9. This individual difference variable was also found to vary greatly across the three classroom contexts

Move 2a
(finding)

---

10. Although different from previous studies, which revealed certain antecedents of WTC, this study posited factors that influenced willingness to communicate in the classroom from the point of view of learners.	Move 3a (significance)

This is a very clear and logical summary. It offers more than a list of findings. As you can see from the moves included, it begins with a restatement of the key aims (sentences 1–2) and some of the key methodological features (sentences 3–4) of the study as reminder before announcing that, despite limitations (sentence 5), the study made some noteworthy findings. These are then summarized (sentences 6–9) before the section concludes with a statement of their significance (sentence 10). Some authors may choose to present this information in two sections, one entitled 'aims and methods' and the other 'key findings'. Other authors may decide to dispense with the restatement of aims and method and devote more time to an expanded statement on the findings. A summary of the key findings will aid the reader's memory, particularly if they have read several chapters of results and discussion. Having offered this overview of the key findings, the author introduces her pedagogical implications.

Pedagogical implications

Again, you may wish to carry out your own move analysis of the text in Box 8e below before reading the analysis in column two.

Box 8e Text of pedagogical implications	
1. The results of the present study have confirmed that WTC is a factor that must be recognized as important in second language instruction. 2. Clearly, an increased knowledge of WTC, coupled with	Move 3a (significance)

Box 8e (Continued)

its potential effects on classroom interaction, would benefit individual instructors, not to mention students. 3. Prior experience and knowledge of how to promote WTC in the L2 classroom can assist an instructor in becoming more effective as a communicator and teacher.

4. The teacher could help ensure that the L2 communication needs of the students are accommodated (Baker and MacIntyre 2000, 2003). 5. The teacher should be informed that the trait-level WTC would only bring learners into classroom situations in which communication is likely. 6. It is state WTC however, that is argued to determine whether learners initiate communication in class. 7. For those learners who have positive WTC intentions, but whose state WTC are affected by a lack of opportunity to participate, the teacher should create suitable interaction opportunities for them to take up to increase their actual output. 8. These techniques should engage students in class discussions more effectively, while providing the added benefit of facilitating the formation of harmonious relationships among students.

Move 3b
(practice)

Move 3a
(significance)

Move 3b
(practice)

Move 3c
(justification)

9. It is also suggested that another aim should be to increase perceived competence, while reducing language anxiety, in ways that promote self-confidence in communication among students. 10. This may be effective in increasing WTC and frequency of language use in the classroom (see also Hashimoto 2003), by creating a less threatening atmosphere and a more pleasant classroom environment. 11. Most learners can be active and participative when a suitable environment is available (Cheng 2000).

Move 3a
(significance)

Move 3c
(justification)

12. At the level of curriculum and material design, the teacher should be vigilant in maintaining learners' interest in involvement in language classes, through carefully choosing materials that appeal to learners, and potentially match their content schemata. 13. The teacher should also be advised to choose task types and adapt discussion topics to students' interests.

Move 3b
(practice)

14. What has been identified in this study is the particular situation in which participants preferred to participate in class. 15. It was found that their preferred class organization was small groups of three or four, leading to a conclusion that teachers should arrange more group activities in which learners feel more willing to communicate. 16. It is believed that group activities have the potential to increase learning (Slavin 1990) since students would help one another in groups to stretch the range of language they produce, thus leading to language development (Jacobs 1998). 17. Oxford (1997) also argued that cooperative and collaborative learning would probably encourage involvement by students with high WTC, as well as allowing reticent students (students with low WTC) to feel more willing to communicate. 18. As an extension of this approach, a factor that could make learning more cooperative would be to encourage learners to work together in groups small enough to encourage group members to be responsible for other members' learning, as well as their own (Ehrman and Dörnyei 1998: 247).

Move 2 (finding)

Moves 3a & c (significance & justification)

Moves 3b & c (practice & justification)

In this section, you will notice the recycling of moves and submoves. The author begins with a paragraph on the significance of her findings (sentences 1–3) in order to provide a form of justification for the practice recommendations that follow (sentence 4 onwards). It is noteworthy that each recommendation for teachers is accompanied by a finding, a statement of significance about her finding(s) or a statement of justification for the recommendation. Sometimes, all three are presented (e.g. sentences 14–18). The paragraph divisions signal a different aspect of practice. Overall, the author has presented a thoughtful set of recommendations for teachers to maximize participation in classroom communicative activities. It is interesting that she decides at this point to introduce ideas for further research. The more typical convention is to consider any limitations in the study, thereby setting a platform upon which to make recommendations for further research.

Implications for further research

The text below in Box 8f contains the author's implications for further research. Again you may wish to carry out your own analysis of the move structure of this section before uncovering column two.

Box 8f   Text of implications for further research

1. The results have provided further evidence confirming that WTC is a useful construct for accounting for L2 communication. 2. What the present study has shed light on is that contextual variables were found to affect learners' WTC in class. 3. Identifying the factor structure of the participation variables will help a great deal in specifying when and why people participate in class and what effect that participation has on learning of all kinds.	Move 2 (finding)
	Move 4a (further research)
4. However, the extent to which factors such as class organization, task type, interest in task topics, motivation and task engagement exerted an influence on WTC within the L2 classroom are issues that have not yet been fully addressed in the present study. 5. Further research that would contribute to a fuller understanding of WTC is warranted, and several possibilities are presented below.	Move 3d (limitations)
	Move 4a (further research)
6. Further research incorporating a similar design, and a larger sample size, would be of value. 7. The present study was limited to a very small number of participants, and it was not, therefore, possible to generalize its findings to an L2 population.	Move 4a (further research) Move 3d (limitation)
8. Another area of research would examine variations in WTC at different proficiency levels. 9. The question can be raised: would similar results be obtained if this study were replicated with students in an ESL context at different levels of proficiency? 10. Further research that considers WTC across proficiency levels would be of benefit. 11. The advantage of looking across different proficiency levels would be the capturing of WTC behavioral change that might not be detected at one	Move 4a (further research)
	Move 4b (justification)

level of proficiency during a relatively short study span. 12. Additionally, this information could be useful to assist teachers and curriculum developers to anticipate changes in students' WTC behavioral intention that can affect student achievement. 13. If changes in WTC intentions are identified, program models could address these changes, with the aim of deflecting students' negative intentions so that they can continue to make progress.

14. This study has identified a number of factors that learners perceive as important in affecting their WTC in class. 15. Future research could examine the relationships between those factors identified in the study and the WTC construct.

Move 2 (finding)
Move 4a (further research)

16. Whether different task types exert a differential influence on learners' WTC also appears to be an area requiring further research. 17. Due to the design of the study, which explored WTC in a natural L2 class setting, the same task type (open divergent tasks) happened to be used by the instructor, making it impossible to look at the impact of different task types on WTC in pair and group work. 18. Any further research in this area should, in particular, examine both open tasks and closed tasks.

Move 4b (justification)

Move 4a (further research)

19. Although WTC was found to change over one-month period in this study, the time span was not long enough to document a systematic change in WTC classroom behavior. 20. Extending the research to longitudinal studies over a much longer period of time would provide even richer data and potential for insight into the effects of length of study on WTC behavioral change.

Move 3d (limitation)

Move 4a (further research)

21. Additional research is also needed to combine others' ratings (such as the teacher) and self-ratings to produce more comprehensive assessment of WTC communication behavior (Yashima et al. 2004). 22. To obtain the teacher's view of students' WTC behavior in class would also add strength to the triangulated approach in terms of data triangulation.

Move 4a (further research)

Move 4b (justification)

Box 8f (Continued)

23. The multiple method of research employed in the present study was valuable not only for the rich data it gathered in the research process, but also because it validated observation as a method for examining state WTC, a variable that is difficult to detect through the use of a single self-report technique. 24. Although the self-report WTC scale, a borrowed and very well-established instrument served its purpose in the current study, its relevance for the purposes of this study is questionable. 25. Further research should consider the approach adopted in Weaver's (2004) study; that is, the construction of surveys specific to a particular context.

Move 3a (significance)

Move 3d (limitation)

Move 4a (further research)

In this section, you can again see the recycling of moves and sub-moves. It is noteworthy that for each paragraph, at least one new recommendation is introduced. Sometimes it is preceded by a finding (sentences 1 and 14), a limitation (sentences 6 and 19) or a limitation and a statement of significance (sentences 23 & 24). In paragraphs where a recommendation is provided first, it has been followed up with either a limitation (sentence 7) or, as is more frequently the case, with a statement of justification (sentences 11–13, 17, 22). Thus, on each occasion, the recommendation is accompanied by a finding, a limitation, a justification or a statement of significance, with each of these serving as a form of justification for the recommendation. At the end of the section, the author introduces a separate section on limitations on aspects of the study's methodology.

Limitations

You may again like to do your own analysis of the move structure of the text in Box 8g below.

Box 8g   Text of limitations

I. The most obvious limitation in this research was that of a small sample size, a limitation that prevented a clear generalized statement about the role played by WTC in the L2 classroom. 2. The number of participants was too small to adequately address the research questions or to possibly generalize beyond the context of this study. 3. With a larger sample, including a greater number of culturally different participants, any real differences would almost certainly have emerged. 4. Still, the small population did not negate recognition of the importance of WTC in L2 instruction.

Move 3d
(limitation)

Move 3a
(significance)

5. This study was further limited by the duration of the research, which was relatively short; so that participants were observed over a relatively short period of time.

Move 3d
(limitation)

6. Finally, the research findings of this study were limited by the inherent limitations of the instruments, and the statistical treatment of data collected. 7. In particular, while it was beneficial to employ stimulated recall as an introspective method in the interviews, because of the delay in the use of stimulus, accuracy in the recall of the participants' task performance was harmed.

Except for sentence 4 which introduces a statement of significance, this section comprises a series of 3d limitation moves. Certainly this is a very clear outline of the issues. Other authors might choose to present this before the recommendations for further research or combine them with the recommendations like the author has done in the preceding section. Having covered her main conclusions, the author wraps up her chapter with an overview of the key points that have been presented in the chapter.

Conclusion

With all the analyses that you have done while reading this book, you will have no difficulty identifying the move structure of the final section of the chapter in Box 8h.

Box 8h   Text of conclusion

1. The primary purpose of the present study was to examine the dual characteristics of the WTC construct, namely, the trait-like WTC and the state WTC. 2. It also aimed to investigate the variations in WTC across different interactional classroom contexts over time. 3. Eight students enrolled in an intermediate-level general English course at an Auckland language school participated in this study. 4. Multiple instruments such as classroom observation, self-report WTC scale and interviews were used to collect data.

Move 1a
(aims)

Move 1b
(method)

5. The most useful finding from this study was that WTC could be treated as both a trait variable and a situational variable. 6. The state variable was found to be more influential in determining an individual's WTC behavior in a particular context. 7. The study provided important empirical evidence that WTC behavior could change across various class contexts and over time.

Move 2
(finding)

8. Results from this investigation of WTC behavior in L2 pointed to pedagogical implications for second language instruction. 9. It was suggested that instructors and institutions should be informed of the importance of recognition and creation of WTC in class. 10. Increased awareness may be expected to lead them to take practical steps to create WTC in class. 11. Guidelines were offered for increasing WTC such as creating a pleasant class environment to increase self-confidence, arranging group activities to promote cooperative learning and choosing materials and topics catering for learners' interest.

Move 3a
(significance)
Move 3b
(justification)

12. Further research was suggested to look at WTC across proficiency levels with a larger number of participants. 13. It was also suggested that factors identified in the study as being of importance in their impact on learners' WTC in class require further investigation. 14. Longitudinal studies were also recommended in order to document, more systematically, changes in WTC behavior over time.

Move 4a
(further
research)

The final section of the conclusion reads very much like an abstract. Here we have a linear and logical presentation of five moves without any recycling of moves. This tends to be the typical pattern of the final section of a thesis, but, finally, the choice is certainly yours to highlight whatever you wish to leave your readers with.

SOME KEY LINGUISTIC FEATURES OF A THESIS CONCLUSION

Modal verbs

Recommendations for various types of application and further research tend to make frequent use of modal verbs. In Box 8i below, you can see that the recommendations for pedagogical practice are most frequently presented with the modal 'should' rather than a weaker modal choice such as 'could' or 'may'.

Box 8i   Use of modal verbs in thesis conclusions

1. The teacher *could* help ensure that the L2 communication needs of the students are accommodated (Baker and MacIntyre 2000, 2003). 2. The teacher *should* be informed that the trait-level WTC would only bring learners into classroom situations in which communication is likely. 3. It is state WTC, however, that is argued to determine whether learners initiate communication in class. 4. For those learners who have positive WTC intentions, but whose state WTC are affected by a lack of opportunity to participate, the teacher *should* create suitable interaction opportunities for them to take up to increase their actual output. 5. These techniques *should* engage students in class discussions more effectively, while providing the added benefit of facilitating the formation of harmonious relationships among students.

6. It is also suggested that another aim should be to increase perceived competence, while reducing language anxiety, in ways that promote

---

> **Box 8i   (Continued)**
>
> self-confidence in communication among students. 7. This **may** be effective in increasing WTC and frequency of language use in the classroom (see also Hashimoto 2003), by creating a less threatening atmosphere and a more pleasant classroom environment. 8. Most learners can be active and participative when a suitable environment is available (Cheng 2000).

Thus, the choice of modal will depend on how strong you want to make your recommendation.

Subordination

In presenting limitations of their study, authors often make use of subordinate clauses such as clauses of concession in order to acknowledge a point of difference or opposition and sometimes in order to highlight certain conditions that must be met so that the statement in the main clause can occur. Examples can be seen in sentences 19 and 24 as follows:

> Although WTC was found to change over one-month period in this study, the time span was not long enough to document a systematic change in WTC classroom behavior. (sentence 19)

> Although the self-report WTC scale, a borrowed and very well-established instrument served its purpose in the current study, its relevance for the purposes of this study is questionable. (sentence 24)

On other occasions, authors will present their limitations in simple (main clause) sentences without any subordination. See, for example, the sentences presented in Box 8g. On these occasions, no comparison with other situations or conditions is made.

FREQUENTLY ASKED QUESTIONS

1. What is the difference between a 'summary' and a 'conclusion'?

If your concluding chapter includes a summary, it will usually be a summary of the main findings of your study. A conclusion, on the other hand, is a statement about the importance, significance and contribution of your findings to the field you have been working in. If you have written a separate discussion of results chapter, you are likely to have discussed in some detail the significance and contribution of your findings to existing theory, research and practice. In the conclusion, you will present a more concise account of these ideas and re-emphasize the special contribution that your work has made to the field.

2. Can a conclusion present any new information?

It is unlikely that a conclusion will introduce any substantively new material because that should have been included in earlier chapters. However, you may want to highlight the special contribution of your work and its place within the big picture referred to in earlier chapters of your thesis.

FURTHER ACTIVITIES

The following activities could be done individually, in pairs (with another thesis student or with your supervisor) or in small groups:

1. Choose one of the theses you have included in your literature review. Re-read two or three of the sections you found most interesting and (a) do a move analysis of the text and (b) think about ways in which its structure is similar and different to the one we have analyzed in this chapter.
2. Re-read the whole conclusion chapter of the thesis you have chosen for activity one and (a) identify any moves or sub-moves presented in Box 8a that were not included and (b) think about why the author may have not included them. Are there any ways in which you think the concluding chapter could have been

made more effective? For example, could the author have toned down the conclusions that were offered or presented them in a more confident and assertive manner?

3. If you have written a draft of your conclusion chapter, you could refer to the move and sub-move options presented earlier in this chapter to evaluate what you have written.

FURTHER READING

If you are interested in reading some of the literature that has informed the material in this chapter, you may find the following references useful:

Bunton, D. (2005). The structure of PhD conclusions. *Journal of English for Academic Purposes, 4,* 207–224.

Cooley, L., & Lewkowicz, J. (2003). *Dissertation Writing in Practice: Turning Ideas into Text.* Hong Kong: Hong Kong University Press.

Evans, D., & Gruba, P. (2002). *How to Write a Better Thesis.* Carlton South, Victoria, Australia: Melbourne University Press.

Hewings, M. (1993). The end! How to conclude a dissertation. In G. Blue (Ed.), *Language, Learning and Success: Studying Through English.* London: Modern Publications in association with the British Council, Macmillan.

Paltridge, B., & Starfield, S. (2007). *Thesis and Dissertation Writing in a Second Language: A Handbook for Supervisors.* New York: Routledge.

Rudestam, K., & Newton, R. (2001). *Surviving Your Dissertation: A Comprehensive Guide to Content and Process.* Newbury Park, CA: Sage.

Thompson, P. (2005). Points of focus and position: Intertextual reference in PhD theses. *Journal of English for Academic Purposes, 4,* 307–323.

Yang, R., & Allison, D. (2003). Research articles in Applied Linguistics: Moving from results to conclusions. *English for Specific Purposes, 33,* 365–385.

Appendix

Move and Sub-Move Options

ABSTRACT

Moves	Sub-moves
1. Introduction	a. Provide context, background of the research b. Identify the motivation for the research c. Explain the significance/centrality of the research focus d. Identify a research gap or continuation of research tradition
2. Purpose	a. Identify aims or intentions, questions or hypotheses b. Develop aims or intentions, questions or hypotheses
3. Method	a. Identify/justify overall approach and methods b. Identify key design aspects c. Identify data source(s) and parameters d. Identify data analysis processes
4. Product	a. Present main findings/results of key aims, questions b. Present main findings/results of subsidiary/additional aims, questions
5. Conclusion	a. Suggest significance/importance of findings beyond the research, considering contributions to theory, research and practice b. Suggest applications (for practice) and implications (for further research)

INTRODUCTION CHAPTER

Moves	Sub-moves
1. Establish a research territory	a. Explain the extent to which it is important, central, interesting, problematic or relevant b. Provide background information about the area c. Introduce (and review) aspects of previous research in the area d. Define terms and constructs

(Continued)

Moves	Sub-moves
2. Establish a niche	a. Indicate a gap in previous research b. Raise a question about previous research c. Identify a problem or need d. Extend previous knowledge
3. Occupy the niche	a. Outline purpose, aim, objectives of present research b. Specify the research questions/hypotheses that were investigated c. Outline the theoretical perspectives/positions d. Describe the methodology & design of the research e. Indicate the scope/delimitations of the research f. Explain the contribution and value of the research to the field of knowledge g. Outline the chapter organization of the thesis

LITERATURE REVIEW CHAPTER

Moves	Sub-moves
1. Establish some aspect of the knowledge territory relevant to your research.	a. A presentation of knowledge claims and statements about theories, beliefs, constructs and definitions b. A statement about the centrality, importance or significance of the theme/topic c. A presentation of research evidence (e.g. findings, methodology)
2. Create a research niche/gap in knowledge	a. A critique of knowledge claims, issues, problems associated with move 1 claims/statements. b. A presentation of research evidence in relation to move 2a. c. An identification of gap(s) in knowledge and/or research. d. A continuation or development of a tradition that has been established but not fully investigated. e. A presentation of arguments for introducing a new perspective or theoretical framework (as a result of move 1 claims/statement).
3. Announce how you will occupy the research niche/gap	a. An announcement of the aim of the research study. b. An announcement of the theoretical position(s) or framework(s). c. An announcement of the research design and processes. d. An announcement of how you define concepts and terms in your research.

METHODOLOGY CHAPTER

Moves	Sub-moves

1. Present the procedures for measuring the variables of your research	a. An overview of the methodological approach underpinning the research project
	b. An explanation of the methods of measuring the variables
	  i. defining
	  ii. describing
	c. A justification of the approach and methods
	  i. explaining acceptability
	  ii. citing previous research

2. Describe the data collection procedures	a. Describe the sample
	  i. describe the location of the sample
	  ii. describe the size of the sample
	  iii. describe the characteristics of the sample
	  iv. describe the context of the sample
	  v. describe the ethical issues
	b. Describe the instruments used for data collection
	  i. describe the tools/materials used
	  ii. describe the validity & reliability measures
	c. Describe the steps in the data collection process
	d. Justify the data collection procedures
	  i. highlight advantages and disadvantages
	  ii. justify choice in relation to research aims, questions and hypotheses

3. Elucidate the data analysis procedures	a. Outline the data analysis procedures b. Justify the data analysis procedures c. Preview results

RESULTS CHAPTER

Moves	Sub-moves
1. Present meta-textual information	a. provide background information b. provide references to methodology detail c. provide references forward to discussion detail d. provide links between sections

2. Present results	a. restate research questions/hypotheses
	b. present procedures for generating results
	  (i) present a result
	  (ii) provide evidence (statistics; examples; tables; or figures)
	  (iii) explain what each result means

DISCUSSION OF RESULTS CHAPTER

Moves	Sub-moves
1. Provide background information	a. restatement of aims, research questions and hypotheses b. restatement of key published research c. restatement of research/methodological approach
2. Present a statement of result (SOR)	a. restatement of a key result b. expanded statement about a key result
3. Evaluate/comment on results or findings	a. explanation of result – suggest reasons for result b. (un)expected result – comment on whether it was an expected or unexpected result c. reference to previous research – compare result with previously published research d. exemplification – provide examples of result e. deduction or claim – make a more general claim arising from the result, for example, drawing a conclusion or stating a hypothesis f. support from previous research – quote previous research to support the claim being made g. recommendation – make suggestion for future research h. justification for further research – explain why further research is recommended

CONCLUSION CHAPTER

Moves	Sub-moves
1. Restatement of aims and methodological approach of study	a. restatement of aims of study (research questions/ hypotheses) b. restatement of key features of research methodology & methods
2. Summary of findings	a. summary of key findings
3. Evaluation of study's contribution	a. significance of findings (for theory & research development) b. significance of findings for practical application c. justification for 3a & 3b d. identification of any limitations
4. Recommendations for further research	a. recommendations for further research b. justification for 4a

Lightning Source UK Ltd.
Milton Keynes UK
UKHW022322310322
400877UK00015B/497